Dialogue on the Path of Initiation

Karlfried Graf Dürckheim
1896 - 1988

Dialogue on
The Path of Initiation

*An Introduction to the Life and
Thought of Karlfried Graf Dürckheim*

by Alphonse Goettmann

Translated by Theodore and Rebecca Nottingham

Foreword by George Maloney, S.J.

GLOBE PRESS BOOKS / NEW YORK

First Edition

Dialogue on the Path of Initiation is translated from the French
Graf Dürckheim - Dialogue sur le Chemin Initiatique
by Alphonse Goettmann.
Copyright 1984 Dervy Livres.

ISBN 0-936385-27-8, Clothbound
ISBN 0-936385-26-x, Paperbound
Library of Congress Catalog Card No: 91-77024

10 9 8 7 6 5 4 3 2 1
Manufactured in the United States

Table of Contents

Foreword

To say that we modern human beings are confused and without a center or a ground for our being is to repeat clichés already overworked in the literature of existentialism. Still we see our world exploding and expanding with a frightening degree of complexity and multiplicity. A helpless atom, we are bombarded by myriads of material creations, all threatening to destroy our oneness-in-being.

I believe we can divide all modern human beings into two groups. One group lives predominantly as prisoners of the tangible, fast-moving world around them. A world of multiplicity that produces ever increasing levels of anxiety due to meaningless existence through a lack of inner harmony holds the first group in captivity to an objective consciousness. In this perspective such human beings are the center and goal of their value system, their motivation and moving force behind their thoughts, words, and deeds.

The other class of human beings, always in past and present history representing a minority, looks beyond material existence and continually strives to attain an inner maturity toward their true self. This is a process that demands death to any lower level of self-absorption in order to rise by transformation to a higher consciousness of one's "essential" or true nature in Absolute Being. This growth neither depends on nor provides an increase in worldly knowledge, skill and possessions, but aims at closer contact with supra-worldly Being. This requires a different kind of knowledge, a knowledge that is based on a special kind of experience, penetrates the mystery of Being, and bears within itself the way that leads to Being. It is, as Dr. Karlfried Graf Dürckheim calls it, "initiatory" knowledge. To "initiate" means to open the way to the mystery of one's true nature in union with the inner Center that knows no circumference, Being itself.

I am deeply honored to write a foreword to this book, *Dialogue on the Path of Initiation*. It has been only recently that I have discovered the masterful teachings of Dr. Dürckheim., It was primarily my reading of this present work that gave me in summary fashion the depth and great extent of this outstanding German philosopher, psychotherapist and spiritual guide's personal development as a human being and as an outstanding Christian.

Since then I have read avidly some of his other works, especially those translated into English: *Hara: The Vital Center of Man*; *The Call for the Master*; *The Way of Transformation*; and *Zen and Us*. Much like Father Alphonse Goettmann, the French Orthodox priest who, in this work, acts not as a mere interviewer but more as a true disciple, I too can humbly say that in my life there was a "before and an after Dürckheim." Unfortunately, I never had the opportunity of personally meeting Dr. Dürckheim before his death in 1988 at the age of ninety-two.

A True Master

Yet I feel through his writings, especially this present work which first opened me to his teachings, that I have found a true master. It was not so much that I discovered some new, esoteric teachings. Rather it was a great Amen! as I was strengthened in my own Christian path to seek even more ardently and humbly to live the heart spirituality that came to me through years of study, teaching and writing about this early Eastern Christian approach to the triune indwelling life.

I have rarely met a modern pilgrim and seeker of the divine life as Dürckheim who integrated the best of Eastern and Western Christianity and also exposed the treasure of the Holy Spirit working in the Eastern non-Christian religions, especially Buddhism.

Dr. Dürckheim believed that all human beings in their "essential" or true nature possess in themselves an innate primal knowledge and conscience that can be brought to consciousness. The truth embodied in it lives in the great tradition, itself timeless, running through all places and all times. We meet it in the enlightened knowledge of great sages and masters, and as the kernel of the creation myths and salvific longings of all the great religions.

He is a modern John the Baptist who is calling not only those of the Judeo-Christian background to encounter the triune community of divine life forming the core of all human beings' true selves, but also those who search honestly to encounter God's Spirit of perfect love in the events of their daily living. Vatican Council II, in its decree on the relationship of the Church to non-Christian religions, confirms Dr. Dürckheim's basic orientation.

Initiation and Transformation

In this present work and running through all his other published works, Dürckheim leads his readers along the two paths of initiation and transformation. The path of initiation is a continued process, but begins with a new awakening of one's essential or true nature grounded in experiencing being as the center of life. The goal of such initiation is to achieve a new structure whose every shift and ripple lets the Absolute show through. Experience of the divine always remains a gift and a grace from ultimate being and there is nothing we can do to bring such experience about.

Yet the way to transformation demands the cross of inner discipline and inner attentiveness to achieve a state of mind and being that is a sign of the conscious level of union with life already realized. This path of initiation means sacrificing everything that prevents us from serving the Absolute and unconditionally accepting everything that helps us to do so.

The transformative process along which Dürckheim guides anyone who wishes to follow his teaching is not for the dilettante or for one who seeks some exotic way of transformation without the cross. Here is a solid teacher in the traditions of the monks of the desert in early Christianity, of Meister Eckhart and John of the Cross, but also in the tradition of the advaita tradition of Eastern religions.

It is a joy for me to know that the writings and the person of Dr. Karlfried Graf Dürckheim are beginning with this present volume to circulate in America. He has often repeated in his writings the truth commonly taught in all true religions: that once the disciple has made contact experientially with the inner master, he/she will then discover the outside master to lead one farther. I hope and pray that the readers of this book will discover that master as I have in Karlfried Graf Dürckheim.

George A. Maloney, S.J.

Translator's Note

Karlfried Graf Dürckheim uses several particular expressions to convey ideas central to his views. He refers to "Being" and "God" interchangeably so as to avoid preconceived notions. The recurring expressions "existential being" and "essential being" refer respectively to the mundane, artificial self and to the deepest part of our nature, our higher self, our virtually unknown essence where the possibility of contact with the divine or transcendent being takes place.

The masculine pronoun has been retained to refer to human beings both male and female due to its extensive use in the original French. The reader ought not assume that this outdated language reflects either Graf Dürckheim's or Alphonse Goettmann's viewpoint concerning things divine and things human. Both men are acutely conscious of the vital feminine dimension in human wholeness and in the spiritual journey.

Introduction

This book was born in Rütte, a village suspended a thousand meters in altitude above the hills and pine trees of the Black Forest. In a chalet buried in the forest lived a man who consecrated his life to respond to the eternal question placed before humanity: "Who am I?" His name is Karlfried Graf Dürckheim. And though he died in December of 1988, his message will illuminate the hearts of men and women for generations.

I knew Graf Dürckheim for many years and this testimonial is the expression of a slow maturation and of profound experience that we both wish to share with those who are also in search of the essential. In my life there was a "before and after Dürckheim." Born into the Catholic Church, I sought my true self for a long time both as a human being and as a Christian, desperately pulled toward the call of the Gospel: "Come, follow me." I read hundreds of books, but I did not find. I frequented different seminaries, but I did not find. I threw myself into prayer, action, politics, but I did not find. Like the psalmist, I cried out my despair to God. That is when I met Graf Dürckheim, like the veiled Pilgrim on the road to Emmaus. It was an explosion within me, an eruption. I fell from my horse like Paul on the road to Damascus and the scales fell from my eyes. Graf Dürckheim was for me "THE" master who made it possible to discover the only true master, Jesus-Christ. It was the great turning point of my life.

Through contact with him and through his teaching, I became conscious of the fact that I was desperately searching outside of myself for that which I carried deep within. I had in fact found

Dürckheim's home in Rütte, near the Black Forest

what I was seeking, but too intellectually. Everything was there, but in the form of rational inventory, tests and strategies. I stood before a locked door. Graf Dürckheim was the key that opened the door to experience; my "knowledge" became life, intelligence descended into the "heart," the Word became flesh within in the great vivifying movement of the spirit toward the unique source of all life which is the Father. Now I was discovering experientially the divine Trinity confessed mentally for so many years. From that moment on, the door was wide open. It opened onto a space which gave birth to all the experiences that shook my life afterwards: in particular, it led to a radically different understanding of the Bible and of the tradition, making it possible to rediscover the Fathers of the Church, and I progressively rooted myself in Orthodoxy. After meeting Rachel, my spouse and companion on the road, the path led us to ask for the sacrament of love and the exercise of the priesthood at the heart of the Orthodox Church of France. That is where we ceaselessly discover with amazement that Graf

Dürckheim's fundamental intuition joins with the very core of the biblical message and can deepen in the Church through contemplative prayer, mystical theology, the divine liturgy and life in community.

It is impossible in the midst of such an experience to "put the light under a bushel." One of the first fruits was the creation of "Béthanie," a center of Hesychast meditation founded on the teaching of Graf Dürckheim. Here, in the soil of experience and encounter germinated the desire to make known to a wider circle the powerful call which Graf Dürckheim addresses to humanity. That is how this dialogue was born.

On a beautiful morning in June, my wife and I took the road to Rütte. The old sage was awaiting us. What grace, what joy to speak with him for days and hours on end. We found in his workplace that climate of mystery and serenity which had already seized us upon arriving in the village. But how to describe Graf Dürckheim? Can words translate his extraordinary force and ageless youth, his fiery temperament, his look at once full of tenderness and yet piercing you to your depths, his often overwhelming smile which illuminated his face, his voice in turn melodious and passionate, his bursts of laughter and his humor? No text could ever render the essence of this encounter.

Thank you, Graf Dürckheim, for the marvelous time spent at your side, thank you for the wealth which you communicated to us, thank you for what you did not say but which the intimacy of your presence revealed to us, thank you for the love you gave us and which will always be alive within us.

Alphonse Goettmann

Dialogue on the Path of Initiation

I

"I have called you by your name."
(Isaiah 43:1)

ALPHONSE GOETTMANN: Graf Dürckheim, each time we meet is a great event for me. If today I am a free and happy man, it is because of you. My life has become a journey thanks to the extraordinary impetus you have given me. I would like to ask you: What are the events that have awakened within you the message that you have shared for so many years and which has transformed my existence and that of so many others?

GRAF DÜRCKHEIM: Well, that is a big question! I believe it started very early. Certain impressions of my youth had a deep effect on my life.

It goes back to my early childhood. I underwent experiences that were filled with that quality we call numinous. This is a very particular atmosphere. According to C.G. Jung, the reality that manifests itself in this numinous quality is the basis of all religion. I believe that this word "numinous" has given European psychology another awareness of human nature, touching the very center of the human spirit, the source of our potential and inherent development. It is precisely the awakening of this core, which we could name inner transcendence, that constitutes the heart of all my work; the awakening of this core and, of course, the experiencing of it.

The openness of my soul toward this inner center occurred in early childhood. Many other extraordinary moments followed in my life and reinforced this part of myself. In these special experiences, I was touched by a profound reality that allowed me to understand they were not a matter of feeling or belief, but of a reality much more real than the one that we consider to be the only reality. We believe that the only reality is the one of time and space and, for Descartes, nothing is real except that which can be enclosed in preconceived concepts. But this is only the envelope of something wholly other, which hides the reality of our depths. It is this other reality that has profoundly touched me at each stage of my life from childhood onward, through the war years on the front and the encounter with death, to the overwhelming and definitive experience that showed me the beyond that is both hidden and manifested at the same time. Eventually these were no longer particular experiences, but a kind of perpetual contact, a state that came and went. It is not possible to be permanently open to this reality, but there does come a time when we always feel the call to turn toward its depths.

AG : This is then the atmosphere in which your life unfolded. Can you recall for us more precisely the important events that made such a blossoming possible?

GD : My first experience goes back to the age of a year and a half. It touched me so deeply that I have never forgotten it. I was in the arms of my nurse who was taking me into the mortuary room where my grandmother lay. The atmosphere was striking: the presence of death, the silence and the darkness of the room, an intense aroma of wax. I felt both attracted toward the bed and frightened, repulsed. It all had a quality of wonder and horror. I

Dürckheim and his father in Bavaria, circa 1900

As an officer, circa 1914

felt for the first time the unity of fascination and terror, those two qualities which always characterize the experience of the numinous.

Then, a little later, I remember exactly certain sensory qualities that greatly touched and impressed me: the aroma from the wood of a little house in which were located my sandbox toys. The smell of wood heated by the sun, I can still smell it today, as soon as I speak of it. Or the smell of wet sand in which I played, the sound of a stream beneath a bridge we often crossed; I would lean on the rail to look at it and listen. There was also the crack of the whip, because I had a nice one when I was five years old; its sound made me feel bigger—it was a very powerful sensory quality. And I well understand Teilhard de Chardin when he says that his first experience of God was a piece of iron that he held in his hand. That was God—there, in the quality of the metal.

The great mystery touches us when we receive sensory qualities directly. One of the marvelous gifts of my childhood, which overwhelms me to this day and orients my work, is precisely this fascination with mystery. In the village church of my birthplace, my parents had a "box seat" from which we could see into the sacristy and follow closely all that was occurring on the altar. I understood nothing, but I felt infinitely. I was on my knees, I looked. I listened without understanding. The aroma of the incense, the songs, the graceful gestures of the priest in his wonderful vestments, the ring of the bells, the light of the candles, the crowd in prayer, all this combination of colors, smells and sounds plunged me into a mysterious atmosphere. Something was happening, something very great, very deep.

You see, it is neither images nor thoughts that count in liturgy, but attitude. One must be in an attitude of surrender, then something new can be born and develop within us. It was precisely because the Mass was incomprehensible to me, but charged with mystery, that it held me breathless: the truth is in the ungraspable.

AG : The "ungraspable." This word like many others, "indescribable, invisible, ineffable," is found at the heart of the Orthodox liturgy and invites us to an adoration beyond all useless and impossible reasoning. True faith is found in a disposition of the heart in which the mysteries speak without going through the grinder of reason. This experience of mystery has so filled you that you spontaneously speak of it in liturgical and hymnic terms. It has always accompanied you on the path of your faith and you have helped so many others to understand that there is maturity in faith only through experience. In this sense, you are the "master of novices" for many Christians, including many monks, who are nevertheless professionals in this area. But this is a big subject to which we will return later.

After a childhood rich in experiences, I believe your adolescence was marked by the war of 1914-1918.

GD : Yes. I was barely eighteen years old when I went into the army. There I was harshly confronted with death, which profoundly anchored the experience of transcendence in my life. I remember, it was on the front. The first dead man I saw was a Frenchman in red trousers on the side of the road. In the wide open and fixed eyes of the corpse, I encountered a sort of dreadful sneering that both attracted me and urged me to run away, held me back and chased me along the road until finally, free and relieved, I had the sensation of rediscovering life as never before. Suddenly, life was no longer something obvious, but a supernatural fullness on the terrifying backdrop of non-life.

Death became my daily companion throughout the war. Especially during the battle of Verdun, under a frightful bombardment and in a landscape of craters that was a chaotic cemetery covered with pieces of human bodies. I was never a hero, I was always afraid when I was alone but, as an officer, I never had any difficulty doing my duty when I was responsible for my men. Each time I left an area threatened by death, there rose in me a mighty gratefulness for being alive and feeling myself alive.

I was at the front for forty-six months, not only in France, but in Serbia, Italy, Romania. I was lucky enough to never fire a shot, I never even took out my revolver, and I was spared from having to kill anyone. Nor was I ever wounded, though bullets went through my shirt and my coat. I truly had a guardian angel.

It is in this atmosphere that life as such took on a numinous character for me. I discovered at the same time that it was in facing death that we step forward toward true life. That experience was later a part of my teaching: by accepting death, we discover and receive life that is beyond life and death, LIFE in capitals.

AG : As a priest, I have had the opportunity of accompanying

As an officer, circa 1918

hundreds of dying people to their birth in heaven. Some roared in rebellion or terror, others, who had understood how to "die" during their lifetime, received death with a sovereign freedom. I saw a very sick person make a champagne toast with his family to celebrate the event. It was not a reconciliation with death which, for the Christian, always remains the enemy to be destroyed, but the revelation of the true life that is the Christ himself. It is the joyful hymn of Easter Night: "Christ is resurrected from the dead, through death has he vanquished death, to those in tombs has he given life."

GD : After the destruction of 1918, the great question that animated seeking souls was that of the new man. A decisive experience caused me not to make this question a simple duty in the era of reconstruction, but to put it at the center of my life. What I lived then I have called the great experience of Being. I was twenty-four, and found myself in the workshop of the painter Willi Geiger in Munich. My future wife, Madame von Hattinberg, was sitting on the table, and next to her was a book. I can still see it now. I opened this book and read out loud the eleventh verse of the *Tao-Teh-Ching* of Lao Tzu:

> "Thirty spokes converge upon a single hub;
> It is on the hole in the center that the use of the cart hinges.
> We make a vessel from a lump of clay;
> It is the empty space within the vessel that makes it useful.
> We make the doors and windows for a room;
> But it is these empty spaces that make the room livable.
> Thus, while the tangible has advantages,
> It is the intangible that makes it useful."

And suddenly it happened! Lightning went through me. The veil was torn asunder, I was awake! I had just experienced "It." Everything existed and nothing existed. Another reality had broken through this world. I myself existed and did not exist. I was seized, enchanted, someplace else and yet here, happy and deprived of feeling, far away and at the same time deeply rooted in things. The reality that surrounded me was suddenly shaped by two poles: one that was the immediately visible, and the other an invisible which was the essence of that which I was seeing. I truly saw Being.

In German we would say with Heidegger: "das Sein in Seienden." I saw Being in that which is. And that touched me so deeply that I had the feeling of no longer being entirely myself. I felt that I was filled with something extraordinary, immense, which filled me with joy and at the same time plunged me into a great silence. I remained in this state for nearly twenty-four hours. That very evening we were invited by friends to listen to a famous pianist. I was kneeling in a corner of the room still gripped by this experience. And I believe it has never really left me. I had not yet understood what this was all about. But from that moment on, there was always something else in my life, something that surrounded me, filled me and pushed me forward. I was ceaselessly directed by a kind of inexplicable yearning and promise. It is still with me today. But at the time I did not realize that this was a call, and the birth of a new consciousness. These are things that I discovered much later, but that is when I was carried in this direction. It also gave me a certain courage to live, a certain innocence in relating to things and people. There was suddenly another reality there, an angelic one, which surrounded me from that moment on.

AG : Do you consider this incredible event to be the most decisive one in your life?

GD : Absolutely. On the level of my spiritual development, this was certainly the turning point whose importance I only became aware of much later. At that time, we had formed with my wife and another couple what we called the "Quatuor." It was in the twenties and we had already begun a certain practice: the daily examination of our consciousness, exercises of inner silence and meditation; my first "zazen."

AG : This experience that marked you so decisively is testified to in every era of humanity. It is the moment when we sense our divine spark. After such a "jarring" there is a time when we can only be still and adore. Then the desire to know rises within us, to know those who through the ages have drunk at the same source and have been enlightened by the same fire. Can you tell us what wood you warmed yourself with?

GD : The attitude of conversion which gnawed at me from then on oriented me in a certain direction through everything I came across. It is not surprising that, in this context, Meister Eckhart created such an explosion within me. I could not put down his

Treatises and Sermons which I perceived as an echo of the divine music I had just heard. I recognize in Eckhart my master, the master. I met him through my friend Ferdinand Weinhandel, a member of the "Quatuor," in Munich around 1920. I am not an expert on Eckhart in the scientific sense, nor a theologian. But we can only approach him if we eliminate the conceptual consciousness. There is such a power that comes out of all he says. That immense simplicity with which he speaks of God, the examples he gives, the problems he raises. There reigns in everything he says a certain atmosphere, the reality of the essential, the real in the silence of the beyond, audible only to those who have ears to hear. You know that he was hounded, condemned as a heretic, and that to this day the Church denounces Meister Eckhart. I myself could have been a victim like him. A Jesuit Father whom I know very well has written a review of my book*Meditating-How and Why*. He tried to be faithful to it, but he attacked me by saying why the book is not good for Christians and that there is a great gulf that he believes I must fill. I answered him point by point to show him that he had not understood me and that I felt as though I was in Eckhart's situation, attacked and misunderstood by the Church. In his attack, Father Wulf said that if there is an experience of the divine reality, it is because God causes it. But I suggest that it is not possible to approach God through categories of causality and rational concepts. We cannot apply existential categories to the wholly other, to the transcendent. With the experiences of Meister Eckhart, I place myself on an entirely different level, on absolutely solid ground, on an unshakable reality, the source, the deepest call that truly forms the center of the human being. But this requires a poverty of spirit that invites us to a complete letting go in order to make possible the birth of God in our being.

AG : I believe it would be fascinating to see, and I am tempted to make such a study, how through Meister Eckhart, who is your principle source, you place yourself in the great currents of the Orthodox tradition of the early times. For Eckhart, alone in the Middle Ages with Tauler and Ruysbroeck, has his roots in the theology of Denys the Areopagite who was a beacon for all of Christian mysticism. Eckhart is dionysian in his soul. And this theology has the same approach to the divine as you do. Denys the Areopagite, a direct disciple of the Apostles, invites us, in order to unite with God, to renounce all rational thinking, all sensible or intelligible objects, all that is and all that is not. For God surpasses all being and all science, He is unknowable by nature and "because of this unknowableness," says the Areopagite, "we can only unite with Him beyond all intelligence."

We could cite many others such as Clement of Alexandria, Basil, Gregory Nazianzen, Ireaneus, Maximus the Confessor and, in the sixteenth century, Gregory Palamas who places us face to face with that mystery where there is only silence and adoration. For them there is no theology outside of experience; the true theologian is the one who is willing to change inwardly, to become a new man through a radical transformation that the fathers call deification. And such a theologian calls every Christian to do the same.

Returning to Meister Eckhart, was he the only great encounter for you?

GD : The most powerful, yes. But there was also the encounter with Buddhism through a book by Grimm that greatly impressed me. Then I read Nietzsche with passion: his *Zarathustra*; that whole book is a eulogy to essential being. There was also Rilke, a friend of my wife's, and Else Lasker-Schuler, the famous Jewish poet; Elizabeth Schmidt-Pauly, another poet; the great theologian Guardini; the painter Paul Klee, and all those with whom I found the same melody on different chords. And the question was already rising within me: were not the great experiences of Eckhart, LaoTzu, Buddha, the same one?

AG : How did this inner consciousness and the experience of the beyond combine with the university system that you frequented at that time, and which saw human beings as intellectual quotients, in opposition to all your convictions and research?

GD : After years of philosophical studies in Munich, I emigrated with my friends of "Quatuor" to Kiel where I developed the intellectual instruments necessary for my future work. We lived in community and followed courses together at the University. I branched off from philosophy to psychology to learn the psychological foundations of the philosophy of values. But what a disappointment! Psychology had little to do with the maturation or the new image of man. I wondered how that which is qualitative in people could be expressed quantitatively, and my aversion to numbers and statistics in psychological research has never left me. Of course, in psychology as in medicine, man can be treated as an object by quantitative methods. But what was to be gained there as a student of human consciousness? A wholistic understanding of human beings is not integrated in the formation of the doctor, the priest, the educator, nor even the psychologist. It is not without worry that I see university psychology develop in the direction of the natural sciences, whatever may be the esteem in which their objective knowledge is held. Depth psychology must always fight for its right to be, and an initiatory teaching on being must do so all the more.

After I received my doctorate in 1923 and married Madame Enja von Hattinberg, I remained another two semesters as assistant at the Institute of Psychology at Kiel until this activity became too narrow. I was then faced with the choice of continuing my studies or going to Italy for a time. My decision was made after hearing one day at Marbourgh, one after the other, the very summits of philosophy: Heidegger, Hartman, Heiler, Rudolf Otto and Natorp. The result: a rejection of all universities and taking up the road toward freedom.

I devoted a part of my stay in Italy to the visit of museums, to painting and drawing. But that time was especially marked by work on the philosophy of unity. I was completely fascinated by the reality and the problem that never left me: a unity that holds everything and which, through an inner order, gives birth to forms. It was in this way that the mystery of transcendent being rose in my conceptual consciousness; much later, I perceived it in its trinitarian impetus and under its three aspects: fullness, order and unity. These works incited my old teacher, Felix Krueger, to name me assistant at the Institute of Psychology at Leipzig in 1925. Krueger was at the origin of wholistic psychology taking man as a whole and not as a conglomeration of faculties.

Entering the Institute for the first time, I was completely flustered at the sight of their equipment. I had to be near quantitative psychology for many years, which always focused my aim, and I was continually animated by my secret discovery. Also, in my teaching and seminars, I sought not so much to communicate knowledge as to awaken inner experiences that seemed fundamental to me. I was one of the first to deal with Klages, Freud, Adler and Jung. During this period, the essence of all science of man already seemed to me to be the qualitative experience of his depth. This conviction dominated all my teaching and only intensified when I was named professor of psychology at the Academy of Breslau in 1931.

AG : You just mentioned C.G. Jung. Did you ever meet him?

GD : It was his absence during an international congress of psychology that caused me to go visit him. Like many others, I was scandalized because he had not been invited. Meeting him made a deep impression on me. I can still see him coming toward me, a pipe in his mouth, like a mountain approaching me. I said to him: "Mister Jung, I learned in Japan that when one encounters a master, one has the right to ask a very simple question." And he replied with his Swiss accent: "Well, what do you want to know?"

"Can you tell me what is an archetype?"

He laughed, for he was the one who had introduced the term in psychology. But since he had suggested half a dozen definitions, I was curious to know which one he would give me. At that moment, he answered: "Pattern of behavior." By that he meant a predisposition of our behavior rather than the result of a habit.

In the last twenty years, the work of C.G. Jung and of his disciple Erich Neumann have greatly enriched me. Their theory of self corresponds to my concept of essential Being. For them the true self is the integration of the deep self with the existential one, which alone gives birth to the person. This is what struck me: C.G. Jung has opened the way to initiation. Unfortunately, the Jungians have not continued it.

AG : And did you have any encounters with Heidegger, who lived in a little village next to yours?

GD : Yes, in the years 1949-50, when I returned from Japan. I had already sent him my little book on Japan and its culture of silence. This book inspired him to look into Japanese philosophy, but he told me that to speak of a philosophy, one had to speak the language of the philosophers.

Later, I met the philosopher Spranger who asked me:

"You lived at Todtmoos, near the nichts, the *nothing*?" (Heidegger is the philosopher of emptiness).

"Yes," I answered, and repeated the words of Heidegger, that to approach a philosophy one had to understand the language of the philosopher.

"Oh," Spranger said, "that is a very dangerous statement on the lips of a philosopher whose language we do not understand at all!"

I met Heidegger again twenty years later, when Suzuki, the eighty-year old prophet of Zen visited me and wanted to see him. It was an encounter of a man of the word with a man, who, as a Zen master, is certain that in opening our mouth we are already lying. For only silence contains truth.

These are some anecdotes on Heidegger, but he never had any influence on my work.

AG : Returning to your encounter with Christianity through Meister Eckhart, it is impossible to avoid the question of its supreme source, the Bible. We are born with that book. Unfortunately, the bad catechisms have reduced it to an intellectual study. Yet the Bible has introduced into history a secret dynamism: that of personhood and freedom. In that sense, it continues to be a true ferment in this world. But there are keys missing for deciphering it. All the schools of exegesis and hermeneutics, the

Dürckheim and Goettmann in dialogue at Béthanie

"materialist" and "structural" readings, are scientific and mental, leaving the Bible closed and its wisdom silent. The only criteria that open it to its spiritual meaning are the ones of those who see and not those of the blind: the experience of illumination of the Spirit. In this sense, your work is profoundly biblical and reiterates the invitation of Jesus: "Come and See!", a path of experience and not of knowledge alone.

GD : Yes, that is the reason why Saint John especially attracts me. I read and reread him a great deal. It is the Gospel of depth. I find in him that which makes religion understandable.

During the war, I carried in my backpack the New Testament that my mother had given me. I still have it. It was there, always accompanying me, but I only read it in moments of distress and suffering, repeating sentences or psalms to myself. I know very little of the Old Testament; what always interested me was the experience of those who wrote it, the patriarchs and the prophets. The concept that the Jews hold of God comes out of the experience of their guides, from the way in which they heard the reality of the beyond speaks through them. This is true of all religions. Every image of divinity is originally an extraordinary and overwhelming experience without images, which is both frightening and vibrant with joy. They place us on another level. But later, the experience is projected on the screen of the self and takes the shape of a picture which, through the conceptual spirit, is transformed into something or someone, and is now understood as the cause of this experience when it is actually its consequence.

AG : There is only one step from this process to ideology, dogma, sects and religions.

GD : This is the very temptation of man, his pride. We must never get away from being rooted in experience. That is why the Gospel of Saint John *is* the Bible for me. He is the model of the man called to have the experience of Christ living within him under the urging of the inner Spirit: "I tell you the truth; it is to your advantage that I go away, for if I do not go away, the Counselor will not come to you."

Today, the Christ would say: "Do not project everything on me, go see for yourselves, that is where you will find the Spirit of truth who will teach you what I cannot give you now." We should take with particular seriousness the parable of the vine and its branches where Christ says: "Abide in me as I in you." That is when we enter into this profound reality to which Jesus refers when he affirms that "before Abraham was, I AM." This is not a misunderstanding, but a reference to a reality beyond time and space that is not merely a privilege of the Christian; it is the same reality spoken of by the Zen master when he asks what face you had before your parents were born. He is not questioning you on your previous incarnation, but speaks of the reality within us which is beyond all other realities.

AG : God seems to always speak the same language to all people in every age, the language of the fire of Pentecost. It is received and interpreted differently according to various traditions. Unfortunately, Christians believe they have a monopoly on it and do not think that it is the same God who is "all in all," as Saint Paul says. Did not the early Christians, to their great surprise, see the Holy Spirit also fall on pagans? Today we are witnessing a current that throws our tradition overboard. We see Westerners wearing the yellow tunic with shaved heads, neglecting the giants of their own past, awaiting "enlightenment" while sitting at the feet of a guru. Can these extremes be linked? The Fathers of the Church saw the manifestation of the Word in every truth, wherever it appeared.

Jung, who studied Zen and Yoga, insisted that their oriental form did not work for us. His profound intuition was that the West would have its own Yoga, built on the foundations of Christianity. In this context, you are a pioneer in the West. You lived with the experience of Meister Eckhart and his tradition, and you were prepared to recognize in the great oriental tradition a wisdom that had certain points in common with Christian mysticism.

What was the influence of India on your work?

GD : India did not influence my development. I went there for the first time in 1974 at the invitation of the Minister of Health, guided by my friend Dhingra. What struck me was that at the heart of all that poverty I never saw a sad face. The way in which those people live poverty, suffering and death without complaining gives cause to wonder. It is astonishing to hear: "If it is our karma to live in this misery, we must not try too hard to get out of it, for it is only in accepting our pain that we will have the opportunity to be reborn on other level." This is a religious attitude that is unbearable to the Westerner.

AG : I admire the realization that their great saints have reached in such unacceptable conditions.

GD : Yes! I met beings who made possible some rather extraordinary experiences for me. I think of Ma Ananda Moy. I had the opportunity to come near her alone in a room rarely opened to strangers. I had been asked beforehand, as is the custom, what question I wanted to ask her. "None! I would simply like to meditate near her for awhile." And that is what happened. Ma was sitting before me, a bit elevated, and an unutterable love emanated from her, especially when she placed her hands on my head. I felt an intense, remarkable heat, but nothing miraculous. It was extremely beautiful and touching. She left me with a deep sensation of intensity and fullness. Ma Ananda Moy was so good as to tell me that this time it was she who had received the spiritual gift given by the master to the disciple, either by touch or through the offering of fruits and presents, and she told me that it was something of the Christ which had come toward her. With her faculties of perception, she had recognized in her experience another than

Krishna. When I left her, Ma told me these words: "Don't forget that the drop can know that it is in the ocean, but rarely does it realize that the entire ocean is contained in the drop." That is something to contemplate.

I also had a face-to-face encounter with a sage of one hundred and six years of age who lived in a cave by the Ganges, in the little Benares where the ashram of Swami Shivananda stands, and who died several years ago. But the old sage was not there, and I only found his wife and a cow because he had gone to Delhi that day. I really wanted to meet him and Delhi is a very big city. But with the help of a good friend, I was able to find him. He was beginning a session with some thirty people squeezed into a little room. He sang in a great voice, and the others answered: "Krishna save me, take away my vanity!" At the end, he saw that there was a European among them and asked me if I had a particular desire.

"Yes," I said, "I would like to sit next to the master and meditate eye-to-eye."

He accepted very graciously, looking at me with his magnificent blue eyes, his face radiant with power. It is a very profound experience to have before you a true master and to hold his gaze. I received very much at that moment.

Finally, a third encounter also impressed me a great deal. It was with an Australian who was meditating on a hill near the ashram of Shivananda. We could see him from far away, for he was very large, with an extraordinary radiance. He had written a poem which expressed his situation and which my friend Dhingra translated for me: "He was an artist and God took away his hands; he was a singer and God took away his voice; he only had his feet and he spoke with his feet." Yes, this man was like the sun. He invited us to meet him the next day in his little home with several other Australian disciples. We sang together, side by side. When we were about to leave, he looked at me in silence, and I was pierced by the ray of light which in that instant erupted from his eyes: a ray of luminous love.

These are three great saints whom I met in India, living witnesses filled with the divine essence from which emanates the breath which reveals the presence of Being.

AG : Listening to you, I have the feeling of communing with something immense that has come among us. We are left without words, with an impression of vertigo.

But the time has come to ask you when and how Zen entered your life?

GD : In Japan. When I was sent there in 1937 with a particular mission which I had chosen: to study the spiritual background of Japanese education.

As soon as I arrived at the embassy, an old man came to greet me. I did not know him.

"Suzuki," he stated. He was the famous Suzuki who was here to meet a certain Mister Dürckheim arriving from Germany to undertake certain studies. Suzuki is one of the greatest contemporary Zen masters. I questioned him immediately on the different stages of Zen. He named the first two, and I added the next three. Then he exclaimed:

"Where did you learn this?"

"In the teaching of Meister Eckhart."

"I must read him again," (though he knew him well already).

The second important encounter was with my Master of archery.

One day, a friend introduced me to him. He was a man with huge black eyes and a little beard. He was sitting on the ground and asked me my impressions of these first months spent in Japan. He soon interrupted me and said:

"That's completely superficial!"

"I am aware of that, but how do I go deeper?"

"You must dig deeply at one specific point, then the periphery of the circle will have gained in depth. That is the purpose of archery."

"I have little time, a tiny garden and no Master."

"You need one hour a day, three meters of space and I will be your Master."

We started two days later. That is how I came to understand Zen as exercise. You know that the disciple of archery shoots for three years on a target of straw of one meter in diameter, at three meters in distance. This is of course an inner exercise which has nothing to do with the fact of hitting an exterior target.

Then I met a friend who taught me sitting in zazen. It is under these circumstances that I discovered Zen.

I would see Suzuki from time to time. He later came to see me at Todtmoos. It was in 1954 and I had just received a telegram from the Protestant Academy of Munich asking me to do a conference on oriental wisdom. I took advantage of his presence to ask him: "Master, could you tell me in a few words what oriental wisdom is?"

He smiled and said: "Western knowledge looks outside, Eastern knowledge looks within." I said to myself: "That is not such a great answer..." Then he continued: "But if you look within the way you look without, you make of the within a without."

That is an extraordinary statement! It reveals the whole drama of Western psychology which looks within the way we look without, making of the within a without, that is, an object. And life disappears.

Then I understood that all truth is to be discovered with this wisdom, and my conclusion was: learn to look without the way you ought to look within. This discovery has brought a great deal to my life and to my work. It joins with the wonderful verse from

Novalis: "Every visible surface has an invisible depth raised to a state of mystery."

AG : That is how you gained the conviction that Western man has forgotten an entire side of himself. In proposing zazen to the West, the meditative sitting particular to Zen, you are revealing a universal wisdom, an opportunity for transformation and for fundamental freedom. You offer an experience accessible to people of all countries and of all times. Only a unified human being can fully become conscious of his participation with the divine. And each person names this transcendence according to his religious consciousness and experience. In Zen, it would be "the nature of Buddha," in Hinduism "the Atman," in Christianity "the divine Trinity" revealed by the Christ in the Spirit.

GD : The Westerner has no method for experiencing this ultimate reality. Zazen, which is the primary way of living Zen through exercise, opens a path in the desert of our current abstraction to allow us to advance toward our true maturity.

What interests me in zazen is that without theory or introduction, we enter directly into exercise. Everyone is offered the possibility of sitting anchored in the *hara*—their center of gravity—entering into a posture which puts them into the reality they are after. But it is only accessible on one condition: emptiness. I insist on the importance of this emptiness which is so often misunderstood in the West. It is not a matter of throwing oneself into nothingness, but of getting rid of all concepts, all images. To become, as we say in Christianity, the virgin cup, to free oneself so that the Spirit can come over us and give birth to life. It is the emptiness of all things which becomes the threshold for the experience of the all. It is only the absence of the multiple which opens the door to the experience of fullness. Zazen is a preparation for this openness of our being.

AG : This openness is a state of virginity and the realization of the Beatitudes: "Blessed are the poor in spirit, for theirs is the Kingdom of Heaven. Blessed are the pure in heart, for they shall see God," as well as the call to leave everything, which resonates throughout the Bible, from Abraham to the rich young man: "Go, sell all you have." To be absolutely nothing is to be everything. Perfect poverty is found only when perfect emptiness is perfect fullness. It is also the "innocence of paradise" toward which the Fathers of the desert strived and of which the staretz Zozima became the spokesman in *The Brothers Karamazov.*

But can we be at the same time a Japanese sage and a Father of the desert?

GD : I would say that we should not take the words "East - West" in their geographic meaning. The best picture is that of man and woman. Man is not only man or woman. She is in him, and he is in her, and to the extent that man does not develop his feminine side and vice-versa, he does not become a man but a robot. If the West wants to remain human, it will have to take seriously the Eastern within it, and it is only to the extent that the Easterners integrate something of this particularly masculine force of the West that they will be able to survive.

We can then say that the interest we Westerners now have for the East comes from the fact that the Eastern within us has begun to awaken and says to us: "Listen, my dear, if you do not accept me you will die of suffocation in the high-rises and the concrete jungles which you build with your rational spirit."

AG : Your work allows the integration of the East and the West within us. It is a sign of hope and of new birth for our time.

II

The Greatness and Decadence
of Humanity

ALPHONSE GOETTMANN: Before entering into the details of your message, can you tell us in a few words what is the core of your teaching?

GRAF DÜRCKHEIM: I would answer: It is taking seriously the double origin of human beings, the "celestial" one and the "earthly" one. The West has forgotten this in relegating the "celestial" one to the realm of faith and believing that only the "earthly" one can be the object of experience and practice. The West has frustrated people in their spiritual development. Yet the celestial origin of humanity is our essential being, that which participates with Divine Being and can become conscious of it in specific experiences. We are citizens of two worlds: an "existential" one which is a conditioned reality, limited by time and space, and an "essential" one unconditioned and beyond time and space, accessible only to our inner consciousness and inaccessible to our natural powers.

The destiny of man is to become the one who can bear witness to the transcendent reality at the very heart of existence. To achieve this, we must first learn to take seriously the experiences through which, in privileged moments, being touches us and calls to us. This is the fundamental meaning of all spiritual exercise as I understand it: to open ourselves to our essential being through experiences which manifest it and to enter upon a way of living which allows us to bear witness to being in daily life. It seems to me that the time has come in which the West is awakening to an experience of being and to a practice of the way which is not merely a privilege of the East but an opportunity and the necessary condition for a living religion.

AG : The greatness and decadence of humanity—a cry of warning and at the same time a song of hope. This is the summary of your message.

We must recognize that man today is sick. He has adapted himself to the world to such an extent that he is faced with a dead-end. The mastery of the sciences, technology and organization have made him a captive of this "earthly" world while his deeper reality, the "celestial" one, is beyond the space and time in which he has closed himself. Yet this beyond is nowhere else than in himself. "The Kingdom of God is within you," says the Gospel.

GD : At the moment when man believes he has reached his summits, blinded by success and the promise of his capacities for the future, he has actually never been further away from the truth of life and from his personal maturity. His "worldly" self has seduced him to the extent that he considers it the only source of consciousness, even of objective consciousness. This is why that self is the creator of the great inner schism. The unity of being is broken: the emphasis is unilaterally placed on the exterior, rational pole and smothers the deeper reality, thereby separating us from being.

AG : It is the source of unhappiness, longing and inexplicable suffering, the cause of many illnesses and psychic disturbances, the very loss of the meaning of life. But this is the result of a story which is as old as humanity.

GD : Old, and more than ever contemporary. We are speaking of original sin. Man wants to become god by his own means and to do so he eats the fruits of the Tree of Knowledge. He says: "I am I," or worse yet: "I want to remain what I am." And this begins very early on, around the age of three, when the child says for the first time: "What is that?" This is where the undifferentiated unity with the divine within is broken and man progressively settles into the separate autonomy of his ego.

AG : He distinguishes the good from the bad, as the Bible says, and falls into opposites, fabricating an ideology in which he projects himself. Having cut himself off from life which is beyond dualism, he tears apart the image of God which inhabits him, and creates his behavior according to his own image.

GD : This is the sin which stops life and has no limits. By fastening himself to something both outside and within himself, man suddenly places himself in a static reality opposed to the life which knows no limit.

He confines himself to the petrified universe of concepts, thoughts, and Kant's famous categories: time, space, identity and causality. From this objectifying consciousness, he places himself outside of the primary reality, the true life. Then "death becomes the wages of sin" in the sense that man puts himself on another plane and turns his back on his original country, finding himself in exile. At the same time, death appears as a frightening response for the one who lives sheltered from the very things which would give him true security.

AG : I smile in remembering the little parable of the beetle who meets up with a centipede:

"How do you do it?" asks the beetle, "how do you lift your hundred and twenty-seventh foot at the right moment and move the eight hundred and fifty-ninth without ever making a mistake?"

The centipede, surprised by such a question, begins to reflect upon it. And he finds himself paralyzed, unable to move forward.

A monk of the seventh century, Saint Andrew of Crete, said that "man is idolatrous of himself." This is one of the best definitions of our original downfall. He has turned the power which oriented him toward his essential being, which is at the very depths of his human nature, toward his little self. And in doing so, he separates himself from his source of life and leads an existence that runs counter to his nature. He lives in a lie and constantly represses his thirst for his true self. His life is a death and all that he does is polluted at the onset. He disintegrates himself and the universe along with him—this is original sin. We experience such inner alienation every day. But we have the capacity to transform this state of death into a state of resurrection. Metamorphosis is possible, this is the goal of all your work.

GD: In the end, human beings always remain children of paradise.

AG: God never ceases to call out "Adam, where are you?" in the depths of the human heart.

GD: But we "do not have ears to hear." Propelled by his ideas, he only hears the God of the philosophers and closes the door to being which continues to call him and search for him. Yet original sin is also the original opportunity for humanity, that which allows us to become conscious of the divine. The goal of life is to recover this deep awareness, for there is no human maturity without the fusion of these two poles. The union of man with his depths, through which he awakens to being and lets it manifest through his existence, is the axis around which our whole life should gravitate. Without that there is no real education, nor serious

With Alphonse and Rachel Goettmann at Béthanie

medicine, and all fields seeking to deal with human nature are doomed to failure. Only this union of the existential self with the essential self, dealing with the whole of man, carries him to his full maturity and bears fruits, the first and most important of which is to be able to say "I am" in the full meaning of the term. This becoming of the "I" and its full blossoming depends on the relationship between man and the world, man and himself, man and Transcendence.

This transcendent "I am" is found at the beginning and at the end, at the origin and in the development of all life. At the heart of all that is, man secretly senses this great "I am" from which comes, and to which returns, all of life. Each being is called to realize in his own way this divine "I am" which seeks to express itself in modalities as varied and diverse as all creatures of the universe.

AG : Like Moses before the burning bush, we suspect His presence, but we will not recognize it until we have, like Moses, taken off the sandals of our self. Don't you think that this is the most important duty of human beings in our time?

GD : Yes, today the most important question deals with the rediscovery of the essential self. It is a matter of liberating the Holy Spirit within us and taking original sin seriously, not as past history, but as the only sin which we never cease to commit. It is vital to rediscover the unconditioned within the conditioned.

Man's suffering comes from being a stranger to himself. That is his deepest agony.

AG : His most personal and most universal pain.

GD : Exactly! For sin has become collective, the result being that civilization in the West has developed only one pole of the human being and has sacrificed the other. Yet man is always called to a double mission: to recognize and master the world in which he lives and for which he needs efficiency, but at the same time to mature on the inner path which is vital to this fulfillment. The fruit of this maturity is seen in a person who is transparent to his essential being, and which he expresses in his daily life.

It is a fact that Western civilization has completely neglected this aspect of our nature. Today, man has no place in education. It begins at school: everything is organized, the child has no creative freedom; very early on he must be careful to make good grades under the threat of not being allowed into college. The little child who is a bit slow, a dreamer, who leans over his work in an almost meditative way, doesn't have a chance. Only the sharp kid, the quick one, is worthy of interest.

University training, in medicine for example, does not give any course on the human being. Everything deals with the body. Most of the doctors of our day base their knowledge on physiology, at best on psychology. A famous German surgeon once said: "In all my operations I have never encountered a soul." But things are changing. In super-modern hospitals there is someone who is on the way and who is beginning to inhibit this approach: the patient. He alone holds personal desires which do not go along with the organization of "teams" that have cut man into pieces requiring specialists. No one is caring for the whole human being.

It is the same for the life of the state: it is a fishnet of laws, commands, ordinances and organizations which leave very little freedom to human beings. Our freedom is reduced to the freedom to accept non-freedom, which is not quite the project God has in mind for humanity.

It is strange that even the Church has not been spared. It has also become an organization from which the theologians, men of science, have eliminated all mysticism.

AG : Eckhart is condemned as a heretic, Francis of Assisi constrained to a rule, John of the Cross thrown in prison, Joan of Arc burned alive. Louis Cognet, professor at the Catholic Institute of Paris, said that one could write a fascinating book on the miseries inflicted upon the mystics by the ecclesiastical authorities.

But theology only became a science in the Middle Ages and the break was consummated by the Renaissance. Yet the Orthodox tradition never clearly distinguished between mysticism and theology, between personal experience of the divine mysteries and the dogma upheld by the church. The aim which constantly dominated the thought of the Greek fathers was deification or union with God to which all Christians are called. Theology served that purpose only. It was not a domain of diplomas nor a career for university professors, but an invitation to mystical experience. The old tradition of the church gave the name "theologian" to three sacred writers: Saint John, the most mystical of the four evangelists, Saint Gregory Nazianzen, author of contemplative poems, and Saint Simeon the New Theologian, singer of union with God.

GD : This is the true meaning of theology which must remain a path of initiation—by "initiation" I mean an opening of the door to mystery. The two poles of this path need to be developed in the West: one is the experience of initiation which deserves this name only to the extent that man feels himself touched by essential being and called to this development which makes him whole; and the other pole which is the means of achieving this transformation. I repeat that the most important issue of our time for Western man is the abandoning of this vision of life directed toward mastery of the world in time and space. We must understand that life has meaning only in bearing witness to essence, to the whole of life which is the Word, the inner, universal Christ present in each one of us and in all things.

Unfortunately, education, including what is found in seminaries, derails man from his spiritual path and from true fulfillment.

AG : It is important to become conscious of the fact that no new structure, no revolution will change man: a new world can only be born from a new man. The younger generations feel this very clearly now. We are witnessing a colossal disconnection with political action, especially in North America, and a wild but promising rush toward the soul. In France, May of 1968 was the last effort to recuperate through political means that which was in fact a suffocating cry for being. The hippies were already precursors, then drugs and now the stampede of methods of liberation which confirm this hypothesis. At the very heart of the church, beyond the deviations we've mentioned, there is now the beginning of a return to the source.

GD : That is because we are realizing that it is the mystical tradition which touches the fundamental truth. Certainly, it is not capable of building planes and conquering space, but man's true conquest is first and foremost himself. Man today is no longer the man of modern times, but the man of new times. We are in the era of the Holy Spirit. There was first the age of the Father, then that of the Son, and now we are entering into the age of the Spirit where man is becoming independent through the discovery of the divine within himself. This is utterly new.

AG : André Malraux, who was an agnostic, was also a prophet of the times to come. "The twenty-first century," he said, "will be a spiritual century or will not be at all." Could you elaborate on that?

GD : The age of the Father is that of man submitting to orders, to the laws of God the Father, the reign of the Father which has been more or less the way of the Catholic church. Then came the age of the Son which was no longer submission to the orders of the Father, but awakening to love. The Father-Policeman who frightens us becomes the Father-Love revealed by the Son, so that from being slaves we become sons of God in freedom.

We are entering today into the times announced by the Christ Himself: "I will not leave you desolate. The Holy Spirit whom the Father will send in my name, he will teach you all things." It is the discovery of the Spirit within us which characterizes our time; it seems to me that this transcendence reunites and reconciles the opposites. If the Spirit, the great third one of the Holy Trinity, is the one who assures the unity of the Father and the Son, he also expresses absolute unity in absolute diversity. This immense creative power, which is beyond opposites and the diversity of life, is our own inner transcendence. As soon as it awakens within us, it transports us to another level which is above good and evil. For example, the Christ's requirement of loving one's enemy: the rational self cannot do it, we know this only too well, for it is against our nature; but we can obey this command on the transcendental plane. I believe that there are always two ways of understanding the words of Christ: one exterior and rational, the other inner, experiential and transformative. It seems to me that the Christ has always sought to awaken within us that transcendental plane which is above good and evil.

This is strongly stated in the commandment: "You will love your neighbor as yourself." For the natural mind, "as yourself" presupposes loving oneself a great deal and making a little effort to love the other in the same way. This is an explanation which is both natural and moral. But the Christ wanted to say something utterly different, it seems to me: "Love the other as if he were yourself," that is, find in the other your own essential being, the Christ. There is only one essence, and I believe that as soon as the spiritual or transcendent eye opens within us, we can see in the other what we are in our essence. Then there is a true encounter between two beings rooted in their essential being, an encounter of essence to essence, an encounter with the Christ. That is why Jesus said: "If two or three are gathered in my name, I am in the midst of them." It is He who speaks in all three.

AG : Because we have so often understood the words of Christ from the outside, our relationships are superficial and the true encounter between two people is very rare. One closes off the other in his role. The doctor only sees in the patient a case, the professor sees in the student an intellectual quotient, the boss sees in the worker a money-making factor. The useful and the functional dominate our encounters most of the time, including our most intimate relationships.

GD : It is precisely this existential plane which the Christ invites us to transcend. Then our attitudes change completely. Let us take medicine from among the examples you have just mentioned. The doctor examines a patient. He enters into his problem and little by little it is no longer the illness which he focuses on but the patient himself. Now he finds himself face to face with a human being on another level, not that of medicine but of therapy. The encounter deepens more and more, there is no longer superior and inferior, but two persons who meet in equality and truth, beyond the existential shell. Then a third one is manifested in the encounter. The great third one who now conducts the dialogue, and it is through His presence that problems are seen from another perspective in order to resolve the difficulties.

AG : In the name of this very experience, some rare doctors today dare to say to their patients: "It is I who care for you, but another who heals you."

What extraordinary change would take place if this way of living relationships entered into families, couples, communities, schools, politics.

III

Earth and Sky:
Our Double Origin

ALPHONSE GOETTMANN: You have just expressed a new image of man, breaking through the usual structures of thought. You disrobe him of all his external securities to create a path toward a personal and authentic experience of the intimate meaning of life. You cry "Down with the masks!" The hour of the person has come. At the heart of this tragic comedy in which modern man lives, you propose your own anthropology. Can you expand on that?

GRAF DÜRCKHEIM: There are two kinds of anthropologies. The one of the universities which studies the evolution of man from his origins to the arrival of today's conceptual consciousness. It sees man as an objective reality composed of three poles: the body, the soul and the spirit. There we find his gifts and faculties as well as the different stages of his growth, so well described by Jean Gebser: the magic stage, the mythic stage, the mental stage, etc. But that vision does not look at man who suffers, who seeks joy, pleasure, happiness. We don't find there the one who seeks a meaning to his life, who loves or hates, who wants to live or kill. The inner man does not exist. The question of the being and becoming of a human being escapes them.

My anthropology sees man as a being conscious of himself, suffering first of all from not being what he is in reality. This is the man who has overdeveloped his existential self and one day must learn to transcend it in order to rediscover his deeper self. We could say that man evolves through three kinds of "self":

—the "little self" who only sees power, security, prestige, knowledge.

—the "existential self" who goes much further; it wants to give itself to a cause, to a work, to a community, to a person. It can go beyond egocentrism, and that is where it becomes, in my opinion, a human being.

—finally, what I call the "essential self," the true "I" of the individual and of humanity.

AG : What is the "essential self"?

GD : It is our core through which we participate in the super-natural reality of the divine universal spirit. Essential being is the absolute within us, the source of our freedom where the divine expresses itself through an individual and particular form in the world of space and time. Each one of us should be able to say with Saint Paul: "It is no longer I who live, but Christ who lives in me"; for the experience of essential being is the experience of Christ present within us, and the unity which is accomplished in that moment must be felt like that of "the vine and its branches."

For me then, anthropology begins with the conscious being, it is an anthropology of the person. I would add to this notion the law which man carries within and of which Christ speaks when he says: "I am the Way, the Truth, and the Life." This sentence is valid for every living thing: within the flower is its life, its path and its truth. It is the same for man; in his essential core he contains his life and his truth which only realize themselves to the extent that this essential core becomes the law of his evolution. In other words: the original image of humanity is its innate path. The path which a flower takes from the seed to the blossom and finally toward the fruit is the reality of the inner image put to work. It is the path which has a sequence of preordained stages already contained in the seed whose movement is the life of the flower and its truth. It is therefore the law of becoming which is the path, and the right path is the truth of our being. Therefore, when Christ says, I am this or that, he is saying something which is a universal law. Becoming aware of this universal principle launches us very far into the depths of our consciousness.

AG : This consciousness which we have of ourselves finally ends in the experience of an absolute. Only then do we discover the face of Christ as our inner center. Without this experience we fall into myth in which we repeat what we learned in books and classrooms.

GD : We do not have a lived, experiential consciousness. On this subject, when Christ said: "No one comes to the Father but by me," the Christian gives it an easy intellectual meaning based on concepts, objectifying it and seeking Christ on the outside through who knows what sort of imagination. While in reality Christ invites man to leave the horizon of his existential self, to plunge into his essential being—which is the Christ himself—in order to encounter the Father with him and in him.

AG : The origin, the inner source.

GD : This is the reality in which we feel ourselves alive and protected, and discover love. This takes nothing away from the belief of the one who "has yet no ears to understand," as Christ says. Without an inner ear, we are limited in our spiritual development to belief, until the day when we break through the walls of this consciousness and find ourselves suddenly on another level; then the ear of faith opens up.

AG : The tragedy is that belief is simply intellectual and therefore does not transform the person.

GD : No! It does not transform. Belief allows one to become a good man, in an ethical sense, as the Pharisees did.

AG : It is morality.

GD : That's right. It is the result of a little tradition which has formed beings in the accepted manner. Loyalty to experience has become submission to a framework of life and to an ensemble of laws imposed by the community of which we are a part.

AG : That kind of Christianity has only exchanged one law for another. Many believers still live in the structures established by Moses, merely making of Jesus a better legislator. In that case, I would not even speak of community, which suggests precisely an inner dynamism of faith, but of collectivity where the behavior of each person is thought out, anticipated, organized from the outside and which leads only to socio-political action instead of transforming experience.

GD : When we see how many Christians identify themselves with this belief, in particular the religious orders. They have a feeling of guilt, and are afraid of being condemned to who knows what if they take the liberty of letting go, once and for all, of the huge weight of formulations learned since their youth and have confidence in the inner voice they hear within. I received a letter the other day from an older sister superior who wrote: "I am happy to have finally found within me the permission to seek out the divine reality which inhabits me and to find that bit by bit the plaster is falling!" What is this plaster if not a belief dictated by the Church?

Neumann, the successor of C. G. Jung, has written a book on

depth psychology and the new ethic in which he speaks of good and evil and of conscience: the man who is part of a community, having it in his system, carries its presence in the consciousness he has of good and evil. Belonging to his community reduces the member to a consciousness of laws and virtues. His membership status represents the life of the community present within him. The voice of conscience in the member of the community is the presence of the community in the member.

AG : Concerning this subject, we seem to be at a great turning point among philosophers, sociologists and scientists. Friedmann took a risk forty years ago when he said: "We cannot spiritualize, and therefore save this world, without a return to the individual, an effort of the self coming from the inner man." Today, the echo of this statement is being heard everywhere.

GD : Our time requires a mighty leap from us. Indeed, the psychologist Neumann says the same thing. With what audacity he incites us to listen to the "still, small voice" which sometimes whispers to us to do something completely different than what is anticipated by the community, at the risk of wounding it, and perhaps even of leaving it; the courage to say "No" and to feel oneself fundamentally free.

At that moment, this "small voice" represents the presence of being. There is the relative consciousness which is filled with the requirements of the community and there is the absolute consciousness which is the expression of Being and which requires at certain moments a rejection of what the community demands. It is striking to see Christ say to the young man who wanted to join him after having buried his father: "Let the dead bury the dead." What a scandal! Christ requires from this man a behavior which is absolutely impossible in the law of the Jewish tradition, according to which the burial of the dead was a sacred duty. By following Christ, the young man betrayed his community.

AG : Christ turns the established order upside down with his invectives against the Pharisees and overwhelms our consciousness in order to put us face to face with the absolute. Some of his words are, as he said himself, like a "sword" which cuts into that which is dearest to us: "I have not come to bring peace, but a sword." This is inhuman and impossible for the "relative consciousness" of which you are speaking.

GD : It exists. I lived it. Returning from the war of 1914-1918, after four years on the front, I found Germany in a curious situation. All the traditions were threatened with communism, which was a great danger at the time. With the remainder of the loyal soldiers, we became little regiments off to combat the communists. As an officer, I had formed one of these regiments and had prepared the offensive. And then one night, I awoke and heard the "small voice" say to me: "You will no longer be a soldier, that time is finished, you will not got out with your regiment." This voice resonated with such certainty that no contradiction was possible. This was an absolutely impossible situation for an officer. I was bound by my oath as a soldier and now I was called by another voice to betray it. I went to my superior and told him: "I will not go out, I will stay here, there is nothing to be done. I will no longer be a soldier." I had the good fortune to find myself before a colonel at whose side I had fought at the front during very dangerous moments. He knew me and knew that it was not fear which propelled this decision but an obedience to something absolute within me. He looked at me deeply and allowed me to be true to myself. But he could have reacted differently.

One year later, I had a second experience of this absolute consciousness. As the oldest son, I was to inherit the family property at Steingaden, which included the castle and the lands of the Dürckheim counts. I was going through a period of doubt and, one morning, I awoke with this unshakable certainty: "You must not become a proprietor, your path is somewhere else." Confronting this new awareness was the old tradition of my family which was also dear to me. Above all there were the deep links which united me with my father to whom I could not cause such pain, and with my birthplace to which I was attached with all the fibers of my being. But once again, there was no doubt, the absolute consciousness had spoken and I had to tear up these links and follow my own path.

This absolute consciousness is an eruption of the creative and transcendent force which inhabits us. It is a weapon against all external requirements, liberating us from all conformism, taboos, morals and traditional practices imposed on us by beliefs and placing us under the imperatives of our inner conscience.

We are on new ground which has nothing, absolutely nothing in common with the old world. Everything is different and yet familiar for the one who enters into it: his behavior, his relationships, his way of knowing, the quality and purpose of all that he touches or apprehends. He has removed the blinders of a closed world to enter into the vast domain of freedom, where it is necessary to blow up all the security systems and eventually disobey the established order, even abandon all superficial relationships which inhibit the contact with being. It is the first step of the return from exile.

"His kingdom is not of this world," and for such a person everything is movement, eruption, permanent revolution. There is never any ending or arrival. The awakened man can only put up with systems if they move and bring about change, and he fights all that blocks the future.

The path toward being is always dangerous, surprising, unexpected for all, beginning with the one who travels upon it.

AG : My wife and I have also undertaken that path. We were torn between the moral laws, the criticisms "that's not good," or

Dürckheim and Goettmann in dialogue

"that is not done," or "you are not allowed," surrounded by misunderstanding on all sides, and the powerful call emanating from an entirely different consciousness. But nothing could still "the small voice" which was always present within us nor our determination to follow it to the end.

GD : Is that how you found your path?

AG : Yes. A path which led to the Orthodox Church of France at the heart of which we can live our faith in the fullness of its biblical, patristic and liturgical roots.

GD : I knew the founder of the Orthodox Church of France, Monseigneur Jean de Saint–Denis. When I met him, I felt that here was a whole other tradition with something tremendous to be discovered. Monseigneur Jean was full of humor, with such communicative laughter. A prodigious radiance emanated from him along with a rare force.

AG : We consider him to be one of the greatest theologians of our time, not an abstract theologian but one always in touch with the supernatural world, both a genius and a visionary. His intuition was that the restoration of primitive Orthodoxy in the West would undoubtedly be one of the most important events of the twentieth century. Is not the hope of all true ecumenism found in the rediscovery of the great tradition common to all Christian confessions?

I must tell you how grateful I am to you for opening me so powerfully to this path through your presence and your teaching.

GD : It was Christ who came to reveal that we are not the servants of a distant God and subjected to an external potentate, but the children of a Father called to awaken to those living waters of the divine Spirit within our essence.

AG : We have just made concrete the "small voice" through exceptional examples, but what is it in daily life?

GD : He who has "ears to hear" can perceive it in every moment in the smallest of circumstances. For example: we feel the need to meditate, to dive into our inner depths, and at the same time there is a letter to write to someone who is suffering. The two require our presence and we can distinguish between the call of being and the call of existence. What to do? We decide to meditate, and suddenly another center is manifested in relation to which we feel responsible for the decision we have just made. Perhaps it is this center which says: "This time you would have done better to write that letter and respond to the requirement of existence rather than to the requirement of your essential being." There is this "I" whose consciousness is above essential and existential being as the source of consciousness called to unify this polarity within us. It is the mysterious "I", of which no psychology has ever spoken, which distinguishes between essential and existential being and admits or refuses the impulse coming from one or the other. The one who takes up the path of initiation develops inner antennas which allow him to receive the least intonation of this small voice and follow it.

IV

The Qualities of the Five Senses:
Windows on the Invisible

ALPHONSE GOETTMANN: People progressively discover themselves in many ways in the course of their existence. There are the everyday visible things, and those which are less so and which sometimes seem strange or mysterious to us. The first are palpable and fall under the senses, but the second are much less evident. Do we not risk speaking too quickly, naming that which we do not know and falling into a belief we have not verified? My question is: What allows you to affirm that there is an essential Being? What are the proofs if any, and how do they manifest it?

GRAF DÜRCKHEIM: That is a central question. My whole teaching turns around this affirmation—that there is an essential Being. But this is not an exterior reality. Rather it is a reality within us which we can experience.

It would be ridiculous to deny the world and to call it imagination as some religious philosophies do in order to say that there is only the inner reality. That is certainly not the case. But the world in which man finds himself is the world of humanity, that is to say, we perceive all that surrounds us in reference to what we are. A Russian philosopher stated that to see movement in the cinema we need nineteen frames per second. These seconds are pulse beats. Let us imagine then a being whose pulse beats a thousand times faster, and another whose pulse beats a thousand times slower. For the first, that which seems to us like rapid movement hardly moves at all, and for the second, that which seems to hardly move rushes by. So the world as we see it is entirely a function of the structure of human consciousness. We look at things believing that they are as they appear to us, while in actuality they are only the result of how our consciousness sees them: a fly for example has an entirely different sensibility than ours. We are lost when we attempt to reflect on reality without considering the human filter.

There are two ways of considering the existence of humanity:

The first is the way of science which speaks of an objective reality of which it can say something to the extent that it eliminates the human experience. It is an objective reality which can be proved because it is there, external, in time and space. In Paris there is a river called the Seine; that is an objective reality that can be seen. This is the reality of science which can be known through an external experience.

Then there is the inner reality which we experience internally: joy, pain, suffering, pleasure. It is the reality of feelings that are subjective only for science and of which it is suspicious. But there are great differences in this internally experienced reality: on the one hand there are the experiences that are part of natural man, such as instincts, desires and faculties that are part of whole field of natural experiences, both external and internal.

But on the other hand, man is capable of feeling from time to time something exceptional in relation to all that has been mentioned, something extra–ordinary, outside of the ordinary. This is a reality which apparently transcends the frontiers of normal human perception on all levels, a transcendent reality.

As in the sciences there must be the *consensus omnium*, everyone's consensus on the results obtained and the possibility for all to recognize it, so in the domain of the transcendent the opposite is true: the circle of those who "know" diminishes.

AG : Aren't we witnessing today a great turnaround? After the conquest of space, won't we try to conquer transcendence?

GD : Our era is occupied with two kinds of transcendence. The first represents extraordinary capacities or powers that allow man to go beyond the normal frontiers of what he knows how to do, such as telepathy, for example. Soviet materialism wanted nothing to do with this until the day when an officer was able, from his submarine, to converse with an astronaut. Things changed. The experts on telepathy were brought in.

We know today that a mother rabbit in America is strongly shaken when a thousand kilometers away in Europe, one of its babies is killed. We also know that plants react to the spiritual attitude of the person who cares for them. We have photographed the aura of certain plants, a living reality sensitive to the love of the people who surround them.

In all that is living there are apparently connections and, if we know how to experience them consciously, we can acquire transcendent gifts and all these phenomena that are called "psychic." But this is a matter of an external transcendence, something that transcends man's normal view of the exterior. He can do things beyond the normal. We have done it with memory, for instance, when we can remember our birth and even the moment of conception. There is a whole team of psychotherapists in France who heal with the help of this method. In Germany, we practice the therapy of reincarnation where one's previous lives are uncovered.

This is all very interesting but has nothing to do with the second kind of transcendence that aims at the development of the whole man as a human and spiritual being that, in other words, aims at deification.

We speak so much today of the expansion of consciousness. It is as though we had opened an enormous calyx toward the infinite, expanding it always further. But I have the impression that a contrary movement must be added: to descend further and further toward the place where there is nothing and perhaps there we will discover a grain of sand that represents the only thing that counts. It is very simple. "One thing is necessary," these are the words of Christ which are becoming of great importance again today when man is trying to do extraordinary things. We must meditate on Christ's encounter with Mary and Martha. When Martha, "distracted with much serving," asks him to tell her sister sitting at his feet to help her, he replies: "Martha, Martha you are anxious and troubled about many things; one thing is needful. Mary has chosen the good portion which shall not be taken away from her."

It is this "one thing" that we must explain when we speak of the experience of the Divine.

AG : Your distinction between an external and internal transcendence is extremely enlightening. The polluting of experiences which I was referring to relates to this external transcendence that remains on the objectifying level of reasoning powers and the development of faculties that, instead of transforming man in his whole dimension, may actually break him. This is not a spiritual path but an inflation of the worldly self and its habitual ways: seeking power, knowledge, possession. The inner transcendence that makes new creatures of us is of another order, and completely escapes our calculations and rules of measurement because its coordinates are radically different. My question relates to this transcendence that a person cannot get hold of: how can we say it exists and in which way does it manifest itself?

GD : First of all, we should take seriously certain experiences of being. They are of two kinds: the little "touches" of Being and the great liberating experiences. At the heart of every event in this world, we can be touched by a reality that has nothing to do with the world: it is another dimension that transcends the usual horizon of our consciousness. We are suddenly seized from within by something that gives to all that is interior or exterior, to the whole ambiance of our actual state, a particular quality that we call "numinous." These are singular moments where we can feel another life within us and in all that surrounds us, the life of essential Being. The feeling that invades us in those moments can be fascinating, liberating or terrifying, but we always feel the fullness of Being that attracts us. In order to open ourselves to this experience, which is available in every moment, we must first develop a particular attitude that orients our whole person. We then encounter in everything another being and not merely a thing. Whatever the shape of the encounter: a simple color, a sound, an aroma, an object, a countryside, even an abstract con-cept, we are always called by a "you" through all that touches us. And at that contact, we react automatically: it makes us vibrate, rejoice, frightens us or leaves us indifferent, we feel invited or pushed away. But the more our deep self is awakened, the more the face of each encountered "you" changes, deepens, and lets the infinite "You," the light of essential Being, break through the finite "you". From then on, our sight and hearing are transformed. Everything that comes to us is tainted by this gentle breath which calls to us and fills us.

There are generally four areas through which we experience the numinous:

First, in nature: there are few people who have not been touched by nature once in their lives—the silence of the forest, the whisper of the ocean, the scents of spring, the waves of a wheat field, or a starry night. These are all opportunities to go beyond the usual horizon and limits of ordinary consciousness.

Second, every work of art gives to the one who has his eyes and ears open something that goes beyond its natural aspect. This is especially true in moments when the words "it's beautiful!" are no longer enough. Everyone has their paintings, their piece of music that always profoundly touches them anew and makes them feel something extra-ordinary.

Third, eroticism is also a field where human beings can be carried onto another level. Sexuality always has to do with death. In orgasm, man dies for a moment then returns. The two are present in the numinous: fascination and terror. This is the very definition of the numinous given by Rudolf Otto, the great specialist of the sacred. In eroticism, we live these two moments: trembling and fascination. We tremble because we are always afraid of giving ourselves and therefore of dying, and we are fascinated by the new life that flows within us.

There is no question here of pornography, that vulgar enjoyment in which the numinous is absent. This is the animal level that every person experiences at some point. The animal and the divine are side by side in us.

Fourth, worship in which we are invited to kneel, literally or internally, to let go of all that is "me." It is in this letting go, which is human and normal, that a door opens through which the Divine enters. Meister Eckhart says that we need only open the door, for God is always before it and wishes to enter as long as we go out, because there isn't room for both of us.

AG : That is true poverty—when our whole being becomes liturgical, when the "little self" prostrates itself. Then, as Meister Eckhart says, God becomes at the same time the place where He works and the work itself. It is always the same movement: the empty calls forth fullness.

GD : You remind me of the story of a man who said: "You know, I prayed all night, I pushed and pushed and tried to break down this door that separated me from God, whom I felt so near. Finally, I collapsed from exhaustion, and suddenly the door opened by itself. I had only to let go and God entered!"

AG : The Fathers of the Church often said that our five senses were doors that could open onto the invisible, and that is why they hold such a place in our liturgy.

GD : That's right. It is the immediate touch of a life that is greater than we are, and goes beyond the limits of a conceptual consciousness that explains the importance of sensory qualities in all worship. At the beginning of liturgy we find dance, scent, fire, song. We are beginning to rediscover all this today. Protestantism has greatly hurt itself by throwing it out.

AG : Ministers, especially Lutherans, are very inspired today by the ancient Eastern liturgy of Saint John Chrysostom because it addresses the totality of humanity. It is not only the intellect that must be deified, but the whole of human nature, body-soul-spirit. Liturgy literally plunges us into a bath of divine glory, it is a festival for our senses.

GD : Yes. For me, the senses are closer to God than thoughts or rational consciousness. We cannot cheat with the quality of the senses, they are what they are, no more no less, and touch us immediately.

I have used the statement of the Fathers in my teaching that says that our five senses can become doors opened onto the invisible. This occurs on the condition that we know how to remain in a sensation; we must stay there without moving and allow the quality that touches us to break through the surface of our consciousness; that way we leave its objective presence and little by little it becomes part of us: it is the awakening to transcendence, even though its quality is seen from the outside.

The experience of a sensory quality is completely different from its conceptualization. The blue that we see is not the blue that is distinguished conceptually from red. For, as soon as we take hold of a quality conceptually, it is no longer the quality that touches us but its conceptual interpretation, which we have added to it, and which separates us from immediate reality. As soon as we name an experience or explain it rationally, we step back from it and distance is introduced, the reality is no longer the same and life dries up. That is why the mystics have always said with Saint Paul: "See as though you did not see, hear as though you did not hear, touch as though you did not touch, possess as though you did not possess."

The call, the encounter with sensory qualities, touch, smell, sight, hearing, taste have always played a big role in my life. Touch above all, because I use my hands a great deal in my therapeutic work. I *experience* people with my hands. There is an experience in the physical contact with another that is extraordinary, especially if we have understood that we must never touch a body, but take hold of a human being. That is what I always say to my colleagues when they ask my advice. You can imagine their surprise when I tell them: "Never touch a body!"

"What must we do then," they ask, "since we deal with massages?"

I explain to them that the traditional massage touches the body and cares nothing for the human being, whereas for me, it is the human being who must be touched. This is something else, for the hands that know how to make contact between myself and the other person are hands that are very different from the typical masseuse.

In the Middle Ages, it was necessary to break through the fog of traditional images of the body. Today, there is another thick fog caused by our rational consciousness that must be broken through as well in order to take seriously the reality that cannot be understood by the intellect. The person who could awaken his rational faculty at that time was well-balanced; today such a person must become free of it and let himself be touched by the immediate gifts of his heart. Only to the extent that we are able to open ourselves to that which touches our center are we able to encounter our deeper reality, while rationalism shrugs its shoulders and says: "it is only subjective."

I remember one of my protests when I was a student. The professor would say that the sound of Do was 256 vibrations per second; I rose abruptly and said:

"You cannot say that, you can pretend with your reason that when you hear the sound Do, there is a medium which vibrates at that speed, but the sound as such is an entirely different matter."

"Explain yourself."

"The sound Do is a particular quality very different from the sound Re, each note gives a certain ambiance, something which clearly touches you."

"Yes, I understand, but all that is merely subjective. Objective reality is only undulations."

"But I live with sounds, not with these vibrations and these undulations."

"All that is subjective, and the only objective reality is that of the undulations."

In this sentence is manifested the greatness and tragedy of the Western spirit. Because of this pretention, that the undulations represent the only reality, we have developed a science of nature, technology, discoveries in medicine, physics, and all that is the grandeur of the West and is admired by all. But we have sacrificed the inner man; the man as subject is considered merely as something subjective and therefore unreal. In saying that, we lose sight of man in his wholeness.

AG : Fortunately, the subjective is not measurable and as such escapes the laboratories of scientists; perhaps that is what explains their irritation with it. But for the mystics, there does not exist any reality more real than that which they experience inwardly. When we become conscious of the possible depths of the senses, each sensation on the surface reveals itself as a reality that is indivisible from the whole reality; it is an expression of the unity of all that we touch with our senses, the unity of the divine extending everywhere. On this subject, I like the beautiful picture of Aurobindo, who says that each sensation is like a wave: it is short, ephemeral, but is always linked to the infinite mystery of the ocean; the wave is a concentration of the entire ocean, an inseparable part of its immensity. The one who has "eyes to see and ears to hear" discovers the infinite in the finite and eternity in passing time, as the poet says.

GD : It is always one in the other and not one here and the other there. Many young people urged on by the yearning for this unity leave for long voyages and seek out faraway places, which are the existential symbol for the reality beyond time and space. Or when we seek the miraculous and personal powers, this is also a sign that man in his depths is made for something else rather than simply being a member subject to his community.

AG : Blessed is he who has discovered that everything is in him!

GD : Yes. We must first become conscious, be open to the call of Being. At the beginning of spiritual development is the awareness of something entirely different within ourselves. The true spiritual guide is the one who will help us acquire this conscious

Circa 1982

realization by taking seriously certain experiences that we have had in the course of our lifetime.

Some time ago, one of my patients who was in her forties told me her story. During our conversation, I discovered an event from her childhood that seemed of little importance. But I encouraged the lady to dig into her memories.

"You were visiting a church with your mother and you were struck by the extraordinary vision of rays of light coming through the windows. Your voice had a particular sonority in evoking this memory. Try to remember, what was it that especially caught hold of you then?"

"Nothing!" she replied. "It was very beautiful. Why do you ask?"

And suddenly her face lit up, she seemed to relive the event:

"Yes, I remember, it was an indescribable beauty, I was overwhelmed, as though transported into another world, but it only lasted an instant."

I felt that she was clearly reliving her experience.

"I was surrounded with peace, light, security."

Then she became worried.

"Must we take these memories seriously?"

"Yes. It is very important. Try again to search your memory. Perhaps you have lived other such moments?"

We met the next day; my patient had once again a face radiant with an inner look.

"Twice I was seized by some strange feeling. It was during a walk in the woods, after a rainfall. I stopped, attracted by a ray of light caressing the moss. Suddenly, it happened: I was part of the moss and in a fraction of a second I was pierced by light. A great shiver shook me, then peace invaded me. In and around me everything was light, serenity. A little noise pulled me out of my contemplation."

"And the second time?"

"Oh, I remember it very well. I was sitting in a subway, and across from me an old woman was looking at me. Suddenly, our eyes met and her gaze penetrated deep into my being. Suddenly, I went from a shadow state to a state of light. I felt strengthened, unified, as though I would never be afraid again."

"How do you connect these three experiences?"

"It's very simple: I felt the same thing each time."

Suddenly I had before me a radiant woman who said to me in a new voice:

"Now I know what you wanted me to understand."

She was transformed, it was the dawn of a new life for her. Through the discovery of the meaning of these three experiences, she had just recognized within herself the presence of the great reality which travels through and vivifies the little reality. This awakening overwhelms and transforms our whole being down to its roots and opens us to the transcendent.

AG : We all have such experiences, which are real opportunities to transcend the mundane, but we are not attentive to them because we are not used to listening to our inner voice. "Hear, O Israel." God continually cries out throughout the whole Bible.

GD : To be present, and listening. The inner ear is the first sense which must be developed. We must let rise within us the sensory quality, impregnated by the numinous, and identify ourselves with its inner movement until it occupies the whole field of our consciousness.

AG : We should live from it, and not merely seek to understand, explain or interpret it.

GD : It is under such conditions that it begins to transform us. All gifts, all senses must be refined, go from the vulgar to the refined, from the exterior to the interior. Like the glutton who has the chance to become a gourmet, the physical body has the chance to go beyond itself by opening to the ethereal body, and then our heavy consciousness becomes capable of discernment. The sensation of the body in its entirety occurs through the awakening of refined matter which represents the ethereal body. The physical body manifests itself through heavy vibrations and the other through fine vibrations, which compose the long waves. But the little undulations go beyond the physical body in such a way that the man who is awakened to his fine matter feels "good in his skin" only to the extent that he goes beyond his skin. In other words: the sensory qualities move from the surface to the depths. The word depth means much more than intensity; that which is deep is that which engages the whole person; the more our feelings are superficial, the more we are involved with only part of ourselves. Deep within, Being engages the whole man and gives him his true vocation. It is therefore very important to learn to make a distinction between the intensity of a feeling and its depth. There are extremely strong, intense feelings that are flat, without depth, and there are feelings of great depth that are hardly a light breeze and yet touch us deeply.

AG : How does this manifest itself concretely?

GD : In eroticism, we can live a very intense embrace with absolutely no depth, while the very same embrace lived in love transports us to another plane, precisely the one of depth. That is how a very light, almost imperceptible touch of the skin can give you a divine shiver.

There are no experiences of Being that do not carry the quality of the numinous. As you can see, they do not simply come through a superlative event, or through an extremely beautiful, good or pleasurable thing. The simplest thing can take us into another dimension as different as a sound is from an image.

But we do not wander onto the path of becoming transparent without encountering obstacles. That is the second aspect of the problem. The greatest obstacle to essential Being, which is life and creative dynamism, is everything that is static, opposed to all change, all development. This is the existential self that can be defined as an "I" always turning around the static desire to maintain a position. This is undoubtedly the simplest definition of the "self" opposed to Being; it is only interested in one thing: to maintain its position at every moment, whether it be a material position, a reputation in society, a role in the social hierarchy, prestige, finances, health—all that ultimately assures a certain security, a certain pleasure in the face of life's changes. This is a great obstacle for a person who seeks to bear witness to essence.

This predominance of the existential self must disappear—the evolution of humanity depends on it. By educating ourselves to this transformation we become apprentices of suffering. The more the established self refuses to suffer, the more we must view suffering as an opportunity on the inner path. The person who is rooted in essential Being knows very well that all that is black also has a white side to it, that all suffering is a sign of possible health or happiness. Health is only that which was sick; life is only that which has come near death, and no one has true life unless he has accepted death.

AG : Shadow and light always go in pairs. The Mother, companion to Aurobindo, insists among her disciples: "If you discover a very thick and deep shadow, be sure that there is, somewhere within you, a great light. You must learn to use one to reach the other." Aurobindo calls it the "dark half of truth." In the East, this theme is well known: at the center of all our darkness there is a sun; at the heart of all our ills there is an opposite mystery. Each element, however obscure it may be, even the most grotesque mistake, contains "depths of truth." We must pass from one to the other. In Christianity, this passage, this "easter" takes the shape of the cross, but—as we have too often forgotten in the West—it is a transfigured cross. The free acceptance of death opens onto resurrection, the two are indivisible.

GD : Yes. All the initiatory traditions speak of it. The realization of Being always comes through a death. But only the person who knows something about death and has had experience of it is capable of speaking about life, of giving and teaching life. This death includes all the deaths of our daily life: each loss that we accept, each link that is broken or that must be broken, each renunciation chosen or imposed, and a thousand other deaths. This is a whole education, an asceticism that is the foundation of this development, of this path of initiation.

V

From Death to Life:
The Breakthrough of Being

GRAF DÜRCKHEIM: The experiences of the numinous can often remain subtle, whereas the great experience of Being creates a radical turning around in the person who lives it; the old world crumbles and a new life is born within him. This is positive transcendence, resulting in rare and wondrous experiences.

Children will go to an attic or a basement to be frightened, to feel something which gives them a shiver. Adolescents like to lose themselves in the woods to feel that which attracts and repels them. Certain audacious adults also seek out danger: for example, the race driver or the mountain climber both seek a nearness to death, to destruction, to feel that which cannot be destroyed. The attraction of danger is the experience of the indestructible; it is in the presence of death that we experience the extraordinary premonition of something that cannot be destroyed.

I know a young lady who took drugs to kill herself. She was saved, and told me one day:

"You know, I will do it again."

"Why?"

"The moment after having taken the poison was so beautiful, I felt such freedom that it was worth it all. It was more beautiful than the whole life I had lived, and I would do it again."

There is clearly a moment between life and death in which millions of people have felt something that, from then on, becomes the most sacred core of their lives. For such people, this can be the beginning of a new life, its measure and criteria, discovered at the moment when they have gone beyond death.

ALPHONSE GOETTMANN: Is this joy and renewal the consequence of letting go?

GD : Let's say that all that keeps you attached to life has disappeared. This is the great letting go. The self that has hardened and the barrier that separates us from the divine have melted. Yet we must never forget that without such a separation we could not become conscious of the divine. We should condemn neither the self nor original sin: there are faults that cause the discovery of what is right; there are lies without which we would never find truth; there are weaknesses without which we would never know what power is; and there are falls without which we would never know what it means to get up again. In the end, everything is connected and one doesn't happen without the other. As you stated, this is the image of the shadows that have not understood the light radiating within them. We must not say that because there are shadows, we cannot see the light. The shadows themselves hold the repressed light, just as each death anticipates life, and no suffering would have meaning without the hope for healing. One is always within the other. What is important in those extraordinary moments in which someone has gone beyond human life is that he is beyond what is generally called life and death. It is neither life nor death. But what is it that goes beyond life and death, affirmation and destruction? It is the state that transcends opposites.

AG : This is a state which the world must have access to since everyone suffers and "even creation groans in travail" as Saint Paul says. At the very moment when Christ dies on the cross, the temple veil is torn, and the crowd suddenly finds itself in touch with the Holy of Holies, beholding the immense freedom to which it is henceforth invited. But suffering had to be unmasked and the abyss of death had to be overcome so that the supreme night could become supreme light. This is the "Lost Secret" to be found in all traditions. "Night and Day are two sisters who have the same love, the Sun," as is written in Hindu scriptures. Shouldn't we move forward into the night of our suffering to discover the dawn of the new day which awaits us?

GD : That's it! The more we enter the night of our suffering, the more we find that man is eaten up by three great distresses.

The first is the fear of destruction, the anguish before death and annihilation; man is no longer rooted in the source of life and to suffocate his fear he surrounds himself with a security system.

Secondly, despair before the meaninglessness of life; cut off from the vital inner reality, man builds himself an ephemeral and artificial universe.

The third distress is the utter sadness of isolation, because divided man is alone even though he is made for dialogue. To be able to communicate through every possible means, he creates for himself all sorts of false relationships. There is no human life that is not marked by these three sufferings. Yet if someone has an experience of Being, he is transformed from one moment to the next. He is no longer afraid of death, he accepts meaninglessness and feels sheltered from solitude.

This transformation is the first and greatest evidence that we have been touched by the reality of Being beyond our normal experiences: we are suddenly freed from our usual conditioning.

If you ask me what allows me to speak of the experience of another reality, I would answer: "Is there a greater reality for us than that which is capable of freeing us from fear, despair and sadness once and for all, regardless of the circumstances in which we find ourselves?" This is a passage to a new level of being. But it is important to know that having the experience of awakening to another reality does not yet make us awakened persons. I have met people who have had dozens of such experiences but who are far from being awake to this other reality. That requires a continual effort toward transformation.

From that effort comes the second evidence of a transcendent experience: a new sense of life is revealed through another way of feeling, of creating and of loving. It is a call to a new way of life.

This is where the third criteria comes from: the quality of the numinous that no longer manifests itself under the shape of dispersed events but radiates in all its beauty, and makes the smallest object transparent. It is an atmosphere, a presence.

The fourth criteria is verified by the birth of a new consciousness. The consciousness of the mundane self always in search of power, knowledge, and possession gives way to the awakening of absolute consciousness. Remember that there are three types of consciousness: the egocentric childish consciousness born from fear of punishment, hell, and guilt; this consciousness satisfies our primary instinctive needs. The second consciousness is expressed through the voice of the community to which we belong, it is directed by the organization and its laws. Finally, there is a third state of consciousness which expresses the fourth element of a transcendent experience. This state of consciousness is an acute awareness of plenitude, and bears witness to the presence of Being.

The fifth proof of the validity of such an experience may lead one to smile or shrug one's shoulders. This is the appearance of the Adversary—the Devil. There, where life is born, the Adversary arises; he is the personification of the power that tries to consciously stop or destroy the life willed by God. The more a person is oriented toward the supernatural life, the more the Adversary attempts to turn him away. This is not a pious story, but a fact found in an inexplicable psychological experience. When a person seeks to have an experience of Being, twenty-four hours do not go by without his being assaulted by an exterior event which troubles or saddens him; the shock comes from the outside and is therefore not a psychological reaction but an aggression, a wound, some bad news, an accident. A good little Christian who fulfills his duties toward his community and believes he is in perfect harmony with his conscience is an easy victim for the Devil, but if this brave Christian comes out of his lethargy and has an experience of God, then the Devil is afraid to lose him and puts everything to work in order to destroy the path of promise.

AG : In summary, the surface consciousness is very fragile and vulnerable, always being bounced about by obscure powers, like a bottle floating on waves. But everything changes when our anchor is tossed into the depths of being which inhabit us. The one who floats in the enormous distraction of his life hears a call and decides to be a seeker. For him there is only one true work, and that is to fulfill the reality of his being—all the rest is only a means to an end.

GD : The motivating force of a seeker is always that which he seeks. The reality he is seeking is always there in his search. He could never search for the divine if he did not carry the divine within him. There are many seekers among us today who have not yet had that experience and do not know what they are seeking, but are haunted by a great longing and desire to find something they have lost. They turn to miracles and to the wondrous, the most direct way to awaken in primitive souls a belief in superior beings. But we should ask where miracles begin. What is there that is not miraculous? The simple fact that things exist, that a color is a color, that a sound is a sound—this is all miraculous. Does it cease to become miraculous because it is known by everyone? And why is it only miraculous when it goes beyond the frontiers of the known?

AG : We need to change the way we look at things.

GD : The way we look at things and the seeing of something are entirely different. We know that the search for the unknown has always fascinated humanity, but instead of digging into himself, man has devoured books. That is not enough, so he runs from guru to guru. That does not satisfy either, so he goes on long voyages, he investigates all the techniques of meditation, and that still does not enlighten him. Today, many sects require incredible efforts and yet do not reveal the divine. There is confusion between technical performance and the discovery of the depths within that comes from letting go of every ambition. Without this letting go, there is an inflation of the little proud self. What publicity there is concerning these so-called spiritual experiences. When a true mystic like John of the Cross, or Teresa of Avila, or a Buddhist saint managed to levitate, it was kept secret. Today, there is money to be made in it, and the mystery evaporates. It's abominable!

AG : We purchase powers and betray ourselves. The Judases have always done business. But living has another price. The person who feels called takes the path and knows that a few dollars and a little leisure are of no help.

GD : He pays the price of a superhuman task and takes upon himself a very heavy discipline which consists of working tirelessly, and finding in each moment the best opportunity for advancement. But he can do this because the divine force attracts him powerfully and his decision is unshakable.

AG : "Narrow is the way which leads to life and few there are who find it," Jesus said. "Whoever does not take up his cross and follow me is not worthy of me." Only those who "leave their nets" and bet everything on one card are worthy. "Who will find his life shall lose it and who will lose his life for my sake shall find it." This is also one of the great central teachings of the *Synthesis of the Yogis* by Aurobindo: "True gift of self, total and without reserve, pitiless erasing of the ego, making of all life the altar of this sacrifice, leads into the vast movement of the Divine Joy."

GD : That is what differentiates it from other transcendental experiences. Consider drugs for instance. The experience of a drug can allow you a glimpse beyond the wall. Because a drug puts the self to sleep, you suddenly go beyond the limits of your usual consciousness. Hashish lets you see colors more vividly and gives the senses an incredible sharpness, while L.S.D., beyond its painful darkness, can plunge you into another universe. The more the experience is "beautiful," the more the desire to repeat it arises. That is where the difference is. The legitimate experience seeks something other than repetition. It gives birth to a knowledge and awakens the desire for an experience always available through discipline but never created in an artificial way. Drugs awaken the desire for repetition that ends in the destruction of the mind, takes away the power to work and ruins their victim. Rare are those cases where the person who experiences the beyond through L.S.D. feels it as a call to enter into the experience through a meditative discipline. But I must also say that drug users often know something which is unknown by those who have not experienced it. And no one can take away this something which they have glimpsed. They have a certain pity for those who do not yet know what there is beyond the wall.

It is no coincidence that, in the fifth criteria, the Adversary of life presents himself through drugs exactly at the moment when the West, for the first time in the history of humanity, awakens in great numbers to the inner life. He says: "You want a great experience? It's not as hard as they tell you. Take a little of this substance and you will have the same thing without effort." And so a part of our youth today falls into the trap of easy experience and misses the path to liberation. It is astonishing that drugs have always existed but that it is only now, when the transcendent is being discovered, at the moment when people feel this yearning for Being and enter upon the way, that the market is full of them.

AG : Humanity is at a crossroad and its choice is all the more difficult now that the Prince of darkness cloaks himself in light. So the experience of transcendence must always be accompanied by discernment. If not, what we believe to be the meaning of life could be absolute meaninglessness, and the path can turn into a black abyss. In other words, there must not be any experience without evaluation.

GD : This evaluation is precisely the criteria we have just considered; it is indispensable if we do not want to wander in illusion and seek to enter into the new Jerusalem whose meaning is infinitely beyond all that we have known until now. If you ask people what is the meaning of life, one will say this, the other will say that. During one of my conferences in Munich where six hundred people were gathered, I asked this question: "Ladies and gentlemen, let's stop for a moment and ask ourselves what is the meaning of life. Let each one answer for himself." Then we all sat in silence. After a while, I stated: "I am sure that many among you have had the following reflection: what a funny idea, that question cannot be asked because the answer is different for everyone, even for each stage of our lives." For one, it is a happy old age, for another it is having children, for a third it is a job they enjoy, another would like an easy death. There are as many answers as there are people on earth. And yet a single answer is valid for all: the person who has truly tasted Being knows once and for all that the meaning of human life is nothing other than becoming a witness to the divine presence in existence. That is the meaning of human life. For me, this is the one answer that is present within all the other answers. Is that not the role of religions, to awaken people to this answer?

In the meantime, man lives in his triple distress as we have mentioned; cut off from his depths and without roots, he is forever confronted with the fear of destruction or death. Projected onto the agitated surface of himself and living in the lies of illusion, his life has no meaning and he falls into the absurd. Finally, the prison of the mind isolates him more and more and cuts off his deep ties with the rest of creation and the source of life. From this condition there arises a perpetual yearning for a life beyond death, for a meaning beyond meaninglessness, and for a love beyond sadness and isolation.

But through a long discipline, or through the gift of sudden grace, the death of the little dominating self can occur, breaking the chains and allowing the incredible experience of Being to seize the whole man. The walls that he had built in the face of fear crumble, his artificial quest for meaning in the face of the absurd runs aground, and his empty affections are transformed. Suddenly, Being reveals meaning to him at the very heart of meaninglessness, and at the very heart of his solitude a supernatural love surrounds him, vivifies him and gives him unity.

AG : This is fascinating. The three distresses come from a deficiency of Being and, when it is revealed at the core of this triple suffering, it unveils at the same time its triple identity: fullness, the light of meaning and love.

GD : Yes. A creative fullness, the light of the universal law that sanctifies all things, gives them a form and a meaning, and unity which restores everything harmoniously. But all that is only theory if it is not a conclusion based on three known human experiences.

We experience power, the creative power within us, something that makes us grow biologically, that makes us capable of working, struggling. In other words, an entire area of human life revolves around this power. This is the power of Being. This is how the aspect of creative fullness manifests itself in the world through a life force, but in an entirely different way according to whether it is found on the level of the existential self or on the level of essential Being. If we are rooted in essential Being, we feel the power of Being in our weakness. God is strong when we are weak, as the Bible says. In absolute weakness, when we can do nothing more, when we are abandoned to death, at that moment we can suddenly feel invaded by a great power in the very depths of our weakness. The power of the existential self, based on what we have, what we know, what we can do is broken, and finally gives way to what we are in the depth of our essence.

AG : What you say reminds me of an interview on television which deeply moved me. It was a conversation with several people who had cancer; their extraordinary serenity made quite an impression. It proves that the beyond is not someplace else after death but exists now within our depths. Its only condition is acceptance in complete confidence.

GD : Indeed. Acceptance is the key which opens the door to life, and that is also true for the two other aspects of Being.

The universal law, which is the second aspect, expresses itself in all that is living, in the energy that pushes a living being toward a certain form that is the meaning of its growth, that which allows it to evolve according to "its way, its truth and its life." To become oneself, to achieve one's unique and particular form, to live in a situation where "things go together," where things correspond to that which seems right and well ordered—this is what human beings seek and without which we cease to be human. This is where the universal law manifests itself, giving us meaning and light. But here again we must consider two levels: the one of the existential self, which gathers light and meaning through ideologies, and that of the essential self where, on the contrary, we receive the light of meaning beyond understanding with our mind. If, in the darkness of unknowing, lost in meaninglessness and torn apart by absurd situations, we are capable of accepting the unacceptable, then we can have the experience of another life. And from this acceptance of the darkness, beyond meaning and meaninglessness, arises the light.

The third aspect, the unity of Being, reveals itself through the same attitude of acceptance. The manifestation of unity is expressed through love. The existential self seeks it constantly through a variety of relationships, whether it be another person, a community, a country or a thing. It must escape at all costs from the solitude which suffocates it. On the essential level, it is precisely at the moment when you are separated from what is dear to you and accept the unacceptable, that a divine love can invade you and give you shelter. Then, in the midst of sadness and isolation, you are suddenly filled with joy and peace.

AG : When we touch the extreme limits of the existential self thrown into the abyss of the three distresses, we sometimes make it over great obstacles and there the floodgates of living waters of essential Being flow into us. But it is also important to know how to hear, outside of these great troubles, the music of this water through the little things of daily life.

GD : The sound of Being resonates all the time. We must learn how to hear this sound. The opportunity of having such an experience is here at every instant, and there are no moments in life when the lightning of Being cannot flash through us.

AG: We can play our own notes or those of Being. It is in accepting to die to our own ways that we can vibrate to the sound of Being. Acceptance is fundamental.

GD: To accept is to live one's death. *Living Your Dying* is also the title of a book from my old American friend Stanley Keleman, a pioneer in somatic philosophy and therapy. He says that throughout existence there are little deaths that must be accepted, and gradually "letting go" becomes second nature. To avoid and fight suffering is natural, but when it comes, we must accept it to receive what is beyond it. That is the case for a lady I know who recently had her left breast removed. Having already lost her mother and her sister through the same illness, she doesn't know what to expect from the years to come. When she awoke from the operation, she said to me: "Now how will I live my life?"

We must accept defeat. Accept it and not pretend that nothing is wrong. We must go beyond the resistance within us with a sort of humility toward the forces that are beyond us. There is a story of two Japanese knights who were fighting. During the struggle, one of them made the other fall from his horse and the man's sword tumbled away from him. The victor jumped off his horse and, instead of killing his victim, he spread out his legs and ordered his adversary to crawl under him so as to humiliate him in the extreme. That is what the knight did, so the one standing picked up the sword, gave it to his enemy, and helped him up saying: "You have won the true combat!"

AG: As soon as we speak of acceptance, most people resist it loudly. They confuse acceptance with resignation, which has been preached for centuries, and which is repulsive to all true human behavior.

GD: Resignation and heroism are two manifestations of the existential self. To accept, yes. To resign, never. We must accept even the darkness within us. I remember a saint who lived on the outskirts of Paris, Father Grégoire, an Orthodox hermit. He had painted a magnificent icon representing Christ embracing Adam in hell. I asked him: "Father, what does this icon mean to you?" And he answered me: "If man recognizes himself in his hell, that is, sees the Devil within him, his meanness, his darkness, his great uncleanness, and instead of pushing all that away he forgives it in love, then the divine can illuminate him. For me, this is resurrection." These are inexhaustible words. By accepting the darkness, a light arises from the shadows. That is the idea beneath "accepting the unacceptable," and is one of the essential truths in Zen.

AG : After a long evening in the hermitage of a Yogi, he told me: "If I were to summarize in one word the entire universe of Yoga, I would say: acceptance." Is that not the fundamental attitude of biblical man: from the "yes" of Abraham to Mary's "yes," God teaches us to enter into this movement of surrender and acceptance; Christ Himself made it the expression of his greatest gift: "May your will be done and not mine. Into your hands, Father, I commit my spirit."

GD : Yes, Christ could not place himself anywhere else than where man hurts the most. He puts himself at the heart of the unacceptable. Not only does he freely accept death, but also the absurd: no one had understood his message and most had rejected it. Also, he did not defend himself before Pilate or Herod or even among his own; without a word, he accepts all humiliations. Finally, he is also in almost total isolation: his closest friends betray him and abandon him. So Christ did not come to take away this suffering created by the world, but to teach us to accept the unacceptable as he did. The cross will be taken away only from the one who has carried it.

AG : This attitude of acceptance is taken up again by the liturgy of the following centuries, which has fed Christians who sang it at the moment of the Eucharist: "He emptied himself, taking the form of a servant." The mystical tradition then continued this way of life, and Saint Thérèse of Lisieux made it very simple and available to everyone: recognize a reality for what it is, accept it and offer it to God. Today, science is discovering how such an attitude can lead to a great freedom. Carl Rogers for example, the eminent American psychotherapist, has made acceptance the foundation of his therapy. This can be found in many other traditions as well. You remind us, however, of an important element in this attitude: the participation of the body.

GD : Of course. You can never accept anything with the shoulders up high and contracted because that is an expression of the existential self that refuses everything that hurts and defends itself against every danger, real or imaginary. We are then on guard. It is only in really letting go of all our tensions that we begin to free ourselves. We will speak later about the importance of the body in what I call the "right attitude" which must become ours regardless of what we are doing.

AG : If acceptance is the transformation of the whole person, body–soul–spirit, we can then understand that it is the key which opens the door to life. The identity of this life, as you stated, manifests itself in all things and everywhere under three aspects: fullness, law and unity. What relationship is there between this trinity of Being and the Holy Trinity?

GD : It's very simple. Fullness of life is the universal life as creative force; this is the Creator whom the Bible calls Father. The law is the inner law which structures, orders, and forms all things and gives them meaning; this is the Word, Christ: "All things were made through him, and without him was not anything made that was made."

The Word is the principle of all formation, giving form to all

Dürckheim near the end of his life

that exists. Finally there is unity which expresses itself in love and reunites in harmony all that was separated; this is the Holy Spirit.

AG : Do you see a link connecting the three?

GD : In life, nothing stops. Movement always leads from the Father to the Son, and from the Son through the Holy Spirit it returns back to the Father. The Trinity is a movement, the eternal movement, the mysterious movement in which we all participate as living beings. Nothing exists outside the Holy Trinity and each living being is an image of it. Life becomes form, and the dynamic unity, which is at the basis of everything that is living links all things; nothing exists outside the Holy Trinity because everything is within it. When this life leaves, things decompose, and a human body turns to dust when it is no longer inhabited by the life.

But, as you know, the Trinity is not a privilege of Christianity. There is no religion without the Trinity. The Christian Trinity is a Christian way of picturing the Trinity of Being: fullness, law and unity; that is, the Father, Son and Holy Spirit. In Buddhism, we speak of Buddha, Dharma, Samgha. In Hinduism, you have Brahma, Vishnu, Shiva. In Shintoism, you have the saber to express power, the mirror to express the law and that famous chain, the jewel that, with its suppleness, represents the gentleness of love.

AG : So what do you see as original in Christianity if we find in all religions that which is the very basis of the Christian faith?

GD : The originality of Christianity is found in the vision of the person, the personal reality, that also represents the goal of human fulfillment: through the possibility of truly becoming a person, one can be deified.

But to respond to the often asked question: "Is there a personal relationship in what is encountered in an experience of transcendence?" I answer: that is a false question. All that touches us and all that we meet, person or object, is felt as a "you," that is, as a being and not as a thing. That is how human consciousness is constructed: whatever we encounter, it is always a subject. But this "you" is far from implying a personal reality. It is the same for the "you" that appears to us in the experience of transcendence. Is there something personal in this "other" that is encountered? The risk is indeed great. In saying "God is a person," we must be careful about once again using a mental category that necessarily makes of God a figure, a closed form, a "person" next to whom there is something else, whereas next to God, there is nothing. That is why I prefer talking about a transpersonal person because that takes away the boundaries. The personal God exists beyond the "you" and I would say that the true person is experienced there where dialogue begins, which is the case when I hear that voice speaking from the depths of my essential self. In dialogue, God reveals himself as an ungraspable Being and calls us to realize ourselves in God's own image and resemblance. This is what characterizes the core of Christianity and makes it unique: man as an existential being is responsible to the divine and manifests the divine as a person. The Spirit seeks to become flesh.

AG : "God becomes man so that man can become God," says the tradition with Saint Athanasius, and "God experiences man so that man can experience God," proclaims Saint Irenaeus. A person is not a knowable quantity but, like God, is an infinite, and if it is true that he is inseparably linked to God, he can only reveal himself in the experience that renders him transparent to Being. In the Gospel, the attitude of acceptance and the "yes" to the realization of the person are constant, but their climax is certainly the requirement to love one's enemies. Then nature goes beyond itself, and man is born into the fullness of freedom. Nothing makes us freer than forgiveness; I believe that forgiveness, beyond all techniques of transformation of the self, is one of the great secrets of passage from an individual to personhood. The staretz Silouan from

Mount Athos said that love of enemies is the only unfailing evidence of transformation. "The Christ is born mystically in the soul at that moment," said Maximus the Confessor.

GD : And we become "one" with Him.

AG : In the Bible, "to know" almost always means a direct experience, an intimate contact, love. Then dialogue becomes a kind of transfusion.

GD : Yes. Because without this experience man will project the image of an independent God in the heavens at the moment when he is touched by Being. This is the result of a tradition taught since childhood, in which man forms the way of seeing, even of feeling and understanding an experience in which he is touched by the wholly other.

On the other hand, in the Buddhist tradition, children are initiated into an entirely different way of conceiving Divinity, and taught to maintain in their consciousness the great void. Then, even if in deep meditation there arises in their consciousness the figure of a man or any other form, they would know that this is merely an image and in reality there is nothing that would allow them to give a human image to God.

AG : Words are both magical and filled with traps. Without them, the experience remains unformed: the experience of the word is a powerful revealer of the heart of God; but we also run the risk of intellectualizing, of putting the divine reality into formulas and of killing the true life! That is why we need both Christ and the Spirit to encounter the Father. Jesus said: "I have come to give you life," and "it is better that I go away for I will send you the Holy Spirit." When the word is crucified, the Spirit brings it to life for us.

GD : That is the great turning point and at the same time the difficulty: in every person, Christian or otherwise, there is the self conditioned by time and space, for which reality exists only in forms. Yet these forms both hide and reveal the universal essence, the reality of all realities, something incomprehensible, invisible, which can penetrate us. The only thing that is important for me is to become conscious of these three forces of the Trinity of Being and to create the conditions that allow us to enter into its movement. This is the meaning and goal of the practice I propose.

VI

"I am the Way, the Truth, and the Life"
(John 14:6)

GRAF DÜRCKHEIM: To create conditions is first of all to speak of technique. Let us not be mistaken about technique, it is not an external thing. As the Orientals say: "Perfect technique is the Tao, and the Tao lived is technique." That is to say that it is already an expression of essential Being.

ALPHONSE GOETTMANN: In this sense, we have already evoked the word of Christ: "I am the Way." So the Christ is the Way, and the Way is the Christ. In this experience, everyone will observe very quickly that a proper attitude of the body is already prayer.

GD : Yet for essential Being to manifest itself fully in a personal form, there must be a transformation of the whole person: body, soul, spirit, for the obstacles are found on all levels and inter-penetrate each other.

AG : If it is true that the body is the visible expression of the entire invisible universe within us, then we can understand that all physical attitudes signify something both psychological and spiritual.

GD : The great theologian Karl Rahner made this wonderful statement: "The body is the spatio-temporal form of the spirit." Because of this, we are seeing a turnabout among Christians, because for many centuries the body was made the principal obstacle on the way and the opposite of spirituality. One had to renounce it and tame it, which is a very curious thing for a religion in which God wanted to make Himself flesh and take on the body of a man. If the body incarnates the spirit, how can we separate it from the person? The body is man in his way of being here in the world. It therefore gathers together the conditions necessary for going toward that which is without conditions.

We have a difficult time understanding this because we always consider the body that we have as an object or a piece of property. But aside from this view of things, we can discover the challenge of a radically different vision: that of the body which we are! In German, we are able to say *korper* for the body that we have and *leib* for the body that we are.

The body that we have is something material, physical, separated from the spirit and the soul. The body that we have awakens within us a particular consciousness which seeks health, effectiveness. It is an instrument which must function well. This body is not us, but on the contrary is an object that must be at our disposal while the body that we are diverges completely from this viewpoint. We could say of the latter that it is our way of being here in time and space, in the present moment. This way of being here includes all of our gestures, through which we express and present ourselves; gestures that are the expression of a conscious-ness absolutely different from the consciousness of the body that we have. The latter is directed toward health and perhaps beauty, whereas the former is oriented toward transparence to our transcendent core. Let's take a simple example: we are having dinner, the food tastes good, we continue to eat and it does not

Dürckheim leading a retreat

bother our health or our looks. We continue our meal and a moment comes when, if we take one more bite, we will feel a little stuffed, a little blocked, abruptly deprived of a contact with our depths; that is when we have sinned against our inner spirit of transcendence. Yet it has nothing to do with our health or our looks. We are cut off from ourselves and we regret that one bite too many. This is an entirely different level than the one of health and beauty, it is a way of being that keeps us in touch with our deepest being, and this attitude forms our consciousness of good and evil in relation to the body that we are. That is why, on the existential level, we can make many gestures, movements, or actions, even ways of talking, which are contrary to the law of the transcendent.

If the body that we are expresses man and his personhood in his way of being here, we can awaken the person through gestures. Let us take an example: people often go to the doctor because of this well–known pain in the shoulders. The doctor, formed by the objectifying science of the body that we have, will say: "Yes, you have cramps, tensed muscles, and I am going to prescribe tranquilizers or even massages. If things don't get better, we will give you shots." This doctor sees the body that we have. But for the one who sees the body that we are, tension in the shoulders represents an attitude of someone identified with his existential self, which is fearful of something. Each tension of the body expresses a fear of the world, of the moments to come that might be disagreeable. We are always on the look-out, we are worried about having to defend ourselves or having to attack someone and not being physically or spiritually able to do so. The strongest contraction is located in the shoulders and the back of the neck. It always represents, as I have said, an outlook of fear toward the world. Whereas the tensions around the heart and the solar plexus represent a fear of emotions; those in the area of the stomach represent a fear of cosmic forces; those in the feet are a fear of the earth and a fear of taking root. Neither medication nor massages will change anything, unless we discover and exercise a confident attitude through the body that we are.

We can say that every illness in man is the expression of a derangement of the person, of the body that we are. Modern medicine is beginning to understand this. We now have psychosomatic medicine, but there again a distinction is made between psyche and soma. We must go further and see the whole person express himself according to his way of being here in his life. If the therapist is himself in a right attitude, the least touch puts his client in another attitude, relating from the body that we are to the body that the other is, and not to the one that he has. Of course, all work done on the body that we are is reflected in the body that we have and vice-versa. All that the doctor does with his remedies has an influence on the body that we are. We must understand that there is a way of being here that expresses confidence, and we must become rooted in that attitude. In my teaching this is learned in a posture, a way of being here in which we are rooted in our vital center known as *hara*. These are the conditions in which a technique can take place.

AG : According to the vision that we adopt, the technique can then be either an asceticism of domination and of release, for the "flesh has desires contrary to the desires of the spirit," or an asceticism of transfiguration, since this same "body" is a temple of the Holy Spirit. In the first case the body will be "a beast to tame," as Lanza del Vasto still suggests today. The asceticism then becomes "mortification" of the flesh. In the second case we will seek rather to "glorify God in our body," to express ourselves again with Saint Paul, and the asceticism will become more of a discipline. But as you have just stated, the work on the body that we have also affects the body that we are. The one who flagellates the body that he has or denies it sweets can some day tame the animal to the benefit of the spirit. As great as the difference is between these two visions of the body for the doctor, so there are points of contact for the spiritual person, I believe. For everything is in our attitude.

Contemplation is, in any case, the royal doorway toward the right attitude, the privileged path and the fundamental exercise of your teaching. Without it there is neither human nor Christian maturity.

GD : Exactly. Meditation and all meditative life which comes from it are the great responses to the invitation of Jesus: "metanoia," or be converted. It is a radical obedience, to be lived on another level than that of moral altruism. It is a breakthrough of the mystery that we are within, and of a free life oriented exclusively toward the manifestation of divine Being. This is not the product of a pious imagination or an object of belief but the result of a total revolution of consciousness that is innate.

The word meditation is found today on many lips and takes on many different meanings. For my teaching, I take meditation in its passive sense: *meditari*, to be led toward the center. In this sense, the word meditation is a generic term that covers, for me, the three well-known phases developed in the Middle Ages: concentration, meditation, contemplation.

To get started on the right path, we must know above all that it is Being which seeks us, that wants to take form within us and that does the work to the extent that we allow it to do so. The divine seeks to realize itself in us, and we have nothing to do but to let it act. The gardener's work is a good example: he cannot pull on the plant in order to make it grow faster, but he must ready the conditions so that this movement, this dynamism of life, will not be blocked.

It is the same for meditation: by creating the necessary conditions, it becomes an exercise of transformation. The first condition is an attitude, as you stated, the right attitude. And for meditation it begins with concentration and proper sitting. When Meister Eckhart was asked where his fine health came from, he said: "From my way of sitting first of all." We can, of course, meditate in any posture and progress, as long as our spirit is in a good disposition.

AG : Sri Aurobindo had replaced the sitting position with twelve hours of daily walking, and Saint Simeon the New Theologian had attained the summits of sainthood flat on his back because his spinal cord was broken.

GD : Thousands of years of experience allow us to say that the posture inherited from the Zen tradition is the most beneficial. We must add that its essence is inherent in the body of Western man as well.

AG : It is inherent in human nature. We like to sit near the earth and do it all the more spontaneously when we have fewer intellectual structures. I have noticed with what ease the mentally retarded sit in lotus position without ever having learned it. In all times, sitting on one's heels in the "tailor" position was familiar to the West and has become, since Teresa of Avila, as traditional among the Carmelites as it is in Japan.

GD : But the Zen tradition reminds us of certain requirements which allow for a quicker entry into the meditative process, eliminating obstacles to the transparence of Being. The importance of the proper vertical position while sitting is especially important. It comes out of a good anchoring in the abdominal region where our center of gravity lies, the *hara* where all our energy gathers. Here everything holds together: the rooting in the lower end of the trunk gives birth to a surging toward the crown, and the supple, relaxed chest allows in turn for the *hara* to manifest. Rooted in the earth, rooted in the sky, such is man's constitution, his double origin.

Escape, sleep and dreaming are a thousand miles from true meditation. It requires submission to a strict discipline, both in the precision of the sitting position and in the firmness of concentration.

In meditation we aim at the "nothing" of the natural consciousness. This "nothing" is as familiar to the Buddhists as it is to Saint John of the Cross, among others. It is not a matter of seeking the empty for its emptiness, but if the fullness of the mystery of Being is to take hold of us, we must leave the agitation of the multiple and detach our consciousness from everything that occupies it.

There has been much debate and misunderstanding about this emptiness. Some Christians only approach objective meditation with the use of a thought or an image and think that the rest is Buddhist.

AG : They have probably not gone very far on the path toward their own inner silence and do not know the meditative way used in their own tradition since its origins. They inevitably confuse the God of Jesus Christ with the God of the philosophers. Yet who gives birth to the Word: the pretty mental constructions of Plato or the silent and virginal waiting of Mary? Saint Paul, in his first letter to the Corinthians, insists with great vigor that we acquire true spiritual wisdom on the condition that we "destroy the wisdom of the wise," that is, if we free ourselves from slavery to the "wisdom" of rational thought.

GD : To create emptiness within oneself, to become a virginal cup, is a vital condition for every Christian. The Word can become flesh in us, but if we are encumbered by the multiple, we cannot "receive it" as Saint John says, "because there is no room in our inn." As long as our consciousness is not freed, we remain deaf and blind, with "eyes that do not see, and ears that do not hear." The representations and mental images of God make of Him an abstraction, and we must be rid of them to go from death to life. This requires a rebirth. For me, meditation has meaning only in so far as it transforms human beings, if the one who meditates comes out different than when he entered into it. If after a half hour of meditation we are still the same as before, then we can be sure that we were in a false attitude.

AG : That explains why so many religious people who meditate an hour or two every day for a whole lifetime find themselves in their old age full of bitterness and unhappiness. "Far from being empty of themselves, they are full... and spiritually sick," Thomas Merton observed.

GD : Unfortunately. We can have some nice reflections on God and even enter deeply with our reason into a word of Scripture without it ever changing us. It is a serious mistake to reduce man to his mind alone. The right attitude will reveal that he is also breath, heart, deep center.

AG : I suppose that after the sitting position, the most important element in the meditative act is breathing. As good Westerners, we have reduced it to a mere process by which we acquire oxygen. But what is it in reality?

GD : We completely miss the issue if we see breathing as only a corporal phenomenon. In reality, it is the breath of the great life, the breath that fills all that lives, and man in his totality: body, soul, spirit. If breathing is not correct, man in his entirety is in chaos. All breathing disorders show a disorder of the person in everything he is and does. Moreover, wrong breathing blocks the manifestation of Being and affects his whole inner development and the whole becoming of the person. Indeed, all bad breathing is the consequence of the little dominating self which has pulled the breath from the vital center animated by the diaphragm and placed it in the upper part of the chest, activated by the auxiliary muscles.

Proper breathing is the great movement of life which, in one beat, gives itself and in another receives itself. Lived consciously during meditation, this movement takes hold little by little of the whole person and transforms him through continual deaths and rebirths. This great "die and become" is the fundamental formula of life present at the heart of breathing, as well as in the whole of creation. This is a process of metamorphosis in which the unilateral domination of the little existential self is abandoned in favor of a new birth and the blossoming of essential Being. It is a true burial of the old man, always to be taken up again, a death to all the rigid forms of existence so as to be reborn on an entirely different level as a person, with all the dimensions which this term implies.

AG : You make me want to sing the hymn: "Open your hearts to the breath of God, His life grafts itself to the souls He touches. May a new people be born. Open your hearts to the breath of God for He breaths in our mouth more than we do."

GD : That is not simply an image or a theory to apply to one's life, but is what happens in the act of breathing when it is properly done. This is what we must become conscious of by living it. This is the great letting go and surrender in exhalation and the regenerated return in inhalation. So man is seized in his totality—body-soul-spirit—by this movement of transparence which, with each breath, contains in condensed form all that must mature on the way. There are no limits to the progress of this movement of transformation.

Breathing is the transforming movement par excellence. It is innate. We must be extremely watchful of the relation between exhalation and inhalation. When we have understood that we must not breathe in, but "let it breathe us in," then we will be able to live our breathing completely. We will first have to pay attention to exhalation, that is to say, to letting go. It is only after letting go that we can receive; inhalation comes of itself. As soon as the inhalation is active and voluntary, we close the door instead of opening it. Inhalation has three aspects in the same movement: openness, visitation and fullness. If you ask someone to breathe out deeply, most of the time they will take in a big breath because they are certain that you must first take before you can give. This is true on the existential level: one must have in order to give, but on the spiritual level, it is exactly the opposite; you must give everything to be able to receive.

Inhalation is always the gift of a good exhalation. We receive it and in this sense it has a double meaning: it is the breath which fills me for the proper functioning of my organism, and it is on another level the "in-spiration," I am inspired or it inspires me. In inhalation, a presence takes hold of me.

AG : The West is used to putting its hands on the most marvelous things and calling itself their owner. It is not surprising that we do this also with inhalation and that we receive oxygen without being vivified. But can exhalation be a voluntary act?

GD : Yes, in exercise it is first a voluntary act, then it comes on its own. We must become conscious of it, follow it and not simply "do it." This is true for all respiratory movement. In general, man's breathing is falsified, and most people breathe from the wrong part of their body, with the chest instead of the diaphragm. This is the result of an attitude of fear and insecurity. As soon as we are agitated, breathing rises to the upper part of the body, we are "outside of ourselves." On the other hand, when we are relaxed and centered, we have right breathing—through the diaphragm—and breathing becomes a movement of the whole person. The first duty in exhalation is to let go, first in the shoulders, that is, to let go as a person and not as muscle. We work on ourselves, not on our body. This letting go in the upper body of oneself at the beginning of breathing is spontaneously followed by a descent during exhalation, a gift of self which becomes a surrendering at the end of the exhalation. Our pelvic region becomes a receptive cup for a new life and we are calm, without fear. As in inhalation, we find again in exhalation three aspects in one movement: letting go, gift of self, surrender.

AG : Surrender is a giving over of oneself, the summit of openness in confident waiting. The moment between exhalation and inhalation is not static but rather opens onto the mysterious living abyss from which is born the inhalation which gives life.

GD : With practice, these two great movements—exhalation and inhalation—become the two poles of a unique movement called the "wheel of metamorphosis": death-birth-relaxation-tension. Harmony between tension and relaxation brings about the "right tension." It is important to see the difference between relaxation and dissolution. Proper tension and relaxation are the two faces of a living being, while contraction and dissolution are two states which exclude each other. The person who is not constantly centered goes from contraction to dissolution: tensed toward the upper part of the body or slouched over, these are two attitudes that lead to death. The Devil, the Adversary of life, does two things: he stops the movement above or below in either hardening or dissolution, two static attitudes that man takes on to the extent that he is closed into his little existential self.

The wisdom of life is a perpetual movement which does not allow a single moment's pause. On the other hand, when the right tension deepens, the breathing movement becomes almost imperceptible; then the source of life, Being, can visit us. This overwhelming moment can lead us to ecstasy or root us within ourselves. But little touches of Being are much more frequent than the satori, the great illumination. One of the greatest Zen masters said that he only had three such experiences in his life.

Exhalation is a leap into the unknown with total confidence and without restrictions, developing the receptivity of the seeker in the extreme, leading him to a radical surrender of all things and making him enter into the mystical night, the darkness of death. Without it, there is no resurrection. This can often take years of practice.

AG : But on the Way, there is more than the dryness of the desert. Sometimes the Burning Bush manifests itself, or the source which erupts from the rock, or an oasis. So many lights and moments of renewal, the forerunners of the great light-illumination. All the Biblical promises can be found there, and those who have gone before us on the Way have lived them.

GD : This should encourage us because it is a tireless work to prepare these experiences, which sometimes last only a fraction of a second, but can become more frequent and deeper. The "wheel of metamorphosis" must turn relentlessly. The false attitudes of the body which block union with Being are progressively eliminated. The tensions and rigidity which always express a distortion of the person are detected and released. Rooting oneself in the vital center destroys all false securities, and a person evolves from a state of fear and contraction to a state of absolutely original confidence.

AG : The one who approaches that shore moves toward a new presence and leaves his old ways behind.

GD : From then on he seeks the inner kingdom of Being. He will learn to destroy deliberately all that is contrary to this way, in particular all the crutches that he is always tempted to return to, be they material, moral or in the order of belief. Yet in all his work, it is first the effort which counts, not the result. And these efforts are made in every moment, not merely in meditation.

AG : When the essential conditions of a technique are brought together—right tension, breathing, centering—and the process of transformation is uninterrupted, the "technique becomes Tao" and the seeker enters into an attitude which Zen calls *hara*. This is the center of gravity located in the abdomen, but is also a disposition of the whole man expressed through the body that he is. Before him now are open stages of maturity on a path with no boundaries. But who can become such a person?

GD : If someone reduces the *hara* to its literal meaning of "stomach," they have not understood anything, because it refers to the constitution of the whole man, thanks to which he gets rid of the predominance of fears and the contracted little self. The person who is in his *hara* is not located in his shoulders, but in a solid base from where he can accept the world and life as they are, in a deep confidence.

The *hara* is the vital center of man; yet the true center will always remain his heart. To keep the heart open, one must never concentrate on it in an objective way, but first learn to feel oneself in one's vital center so as to come in contact with the universal power which inhabits it. As you know, there are two forces in us: the one of the will that we "do," and the universal force in which we participate and that we must learn to receive. The force that we access through the *hara* is an individual manifestation of this universal power which is called *ki.* We have a thousand proofs of this power, and here is a simple example of it: I put my arm straight out horizontally and ask someone to bend it. If I remove my *hara* and pull in the stomach, the other person will eventually bend my arm. If, on the other hand, I let go of myself in my arms and am well relaxed and in my *hara* I let the power rise into my arm and no one will be able to bend it. Willpower has nothing to do with it. It's a very curious thing.

Another example: Sitting on a chair, two men can easily lift you up. If you place yourself in your *hara,* they will not be able to. We still don't know what this is on the physical level.

AG : The Psalmist often cried out: "Lord, you are my power, in you I have placed my confidence... I lean on you." For the one who has faith, can the force of *hara* be connected to the divine presence?

GD : Be careful. The way you ask that question could make the divine reality seem closed. I would rather say: "What is not a manifestation of the divine power?" It is in the divine Being that we have "life, movement and being," as Saint Paul said. Therefore, Being is the true center of all that exists, and all that exists does not realize its inner truth unless it allows Being to manifest itself in its particular form. We can say that man is truly in his center when he has become conscious of his own path as an innate truth and

With a student

as a personal call, and that he is capable of consciously realizing it through the simplest activity in daily life.

As the realization of the way enters into the deeper layers of consciousness, it represents a radical turning around, a total reorientation. Life no longer turns around man but around divine Being and its manifestation. To be centered is then revealed as an extreme sensitivity toward everything that inhibits transparence, and toward all that favors it. This is a state of permanent critical watchfulness which mobilizes a person in his totality.

Here the body in its form, its attitude and all its dynamism is the expression of the becoming of the person on the way to transformation. It evolves between the high and the low, between heaven and earth, and progressively returns man to his double origin: earthly and celestial. The openness to *hara* roots him in cosmic forces and liberates him from slavery to the little self, while opening him to the upper part of the body—chest, neck, head—which roots him in spiritual forces. But it is only when the integration is made between earth and sky that man finds his true center in the heart, there where his personhood comes forth.

AG : Finally, it is neither the *hara* nor the head, but the heart which is man's center.

GD : Yes, the heart not as the seat of our feelings, but as the center which opens when the self has abandoned everything and, open to earth and sky, anchors itself in the nerve-center which links the two together. Physically, this point is found at the level of the solar plexus.

That is where the horizontal and the vertical cross: earthly life, conditioned by all the weight of history; and celestial life, unconditioned, beyond space and time, divine Being. It is only in this tension that the personal center of man is formed; when he allows the unconditioned to manifest itself in the conditioned and strength blossoms in weakness, meaning in meaninglessness, love in the cruelty of the world; when man knows that he can live only from Being, for Him and with Him, and accepts over and over again the responsibility of not betraying it by escaping into the horizontal.

At the heart of this tension, and animated by this incessant movement between the horizontal and the vertical, man is on the cross. But from his center surges the light of the person who is born and reborn. Death on the cross is always inseparable from resurrection, new life. The symbol of the cross is also that of the universal situation of all that exists, containing the tension between supernatural reality, along with the image of the seed, and the conditions that permit it to manifest this image in a conditioned form. So all of creation is itself on the cross.

But there is more: this cross that reveals the center of man and of all things is also the incandescent center of an encounter with the Christ. He is the center of every center and the principle of all form, the Word through which the whole man is in his center, where he feels himself one with Christ, and hears His call as the inner master. His whole life then comes out of Christ.

To say this would have no meaning and would only be a pious belief with little value if it was not a matter of an actual experience and of a transformation, of a concrete path that travels through the pangs of death toward another life.

AG : That is what Jesus lived and he invites us to nothing else. He never sought to indoctrinate his audience with all the little doctrines of good moral conduct. His teaching was "good news" always calling people to the most concrete experience. "Come and see!" are the first words addressed to his disciples and the content of a path not to be "learned" but to be "experienced." The whole problem of current religious education is found here: it is a problem of method. The apostles understood this and were seized by it. In following Christ, their preaching had nothing theoretical in it and was far from being a simple intellectual assent to another dogmatic proposition. The Christian paradox of the cross inter-vened to crucify our understanding. Saint Paul presents the cross as "foolishness," and asks his listeners to accept the unacceptable so that they may feel within them this secret and mysterious power that is the presence of Christ himself. "To be nailed on the cross of Christ" meant, for him and the other Christians, a vigorous experience of death, to such an extent that the little self was no longer the principle center of their actions; henceforth, they proceeded from Christ who lived within them.

The dynamism of this extraordinary theology was evident throughout the golden age of the Fathers. The levers on this path are self-surrender, inner purity, what can be called "letting go" or detachment, and a contemplation eliminating all concepts of God. The realization of this experience was expressed even in the formulation of dogma. The expression of dogma is often paradoxical, contradictory, requiring reason to step out of its closed circuit, to explode in a way and to transcend itself into the mystery that it cannot contemplate. Compared to this, those who call themselves theologians today are most often occupied with religious philosophy.

GD : The system of beliefs that has been built in the minds of Christians has emptied itself and is now crumbling. It is their despair and the agony of our time. They seek an experiential verification of their faith that neither their education nor any dogma has ever allowed. A doctrine has been transmitted to them that completely ignores the awakening to their reality as people and what lies within such blossoming.

AG : Where are the prophets, the masters, those who can awaken us in the churches today? Yet, who does not aspire to hear anew, through the voice of a prophet or of a Church, the burning cry of Jesus: "Come, follow me," and to go after him concretely on the famous Way which the Acts of the Apostles spoke of so often.

GD : You touch here on the very heart of all my efforts. I seek to place myself in the wake of Christ and not in that of the Buddha. My aim is not to propose experiences of liberation or of illumination but their fruit, which is transformation into a true person. Christ has shown us the way of this becoming and has lived it before our eyes. He himself entered on that path, as he said: "Follow me." To do so is to discover his "kingdom which is not of this world." For that, it is indispensable, as you have suggested, to "take up one's cross," to accept the unacceptable as Christ did, the annihilation of the existential self by passing through death, the absurd, solitude and, in surrender to Being, to experience redemption. "He who loses his life for my sake will find it..."

He is therefore the way, but also the life, and to find it one must have let go of everything. "Go, sell all you have, then come and follow me." It is only on this condition that each can realize his own truth, by following the one who is "the Way, the Truth and the Life."

In Jesus, the great life opens its eyes for the first time, in him man becomes conscious that he is himself this great life and is called to manifest it, to let it shine through him in existence. Jesus is the "New Adam" because he is the first man in which the person can be fully seen.

The experience of God made man in Jesus Christ is an awesome event at the heart of history. It is the culmination of a long human becoming, and from this experience of Jesus comes a new history of humanity. From now on, to live in fullness means to participate in this turning point in history by following Jesus Christ.

AG : And the true vocation of the Church is to call each person to live this prodigious experience in communion with others so that, as the Psalmist says, "from sea to sea to the ends of the earth," all humanity sets out for this unique adventure. Then the Church is the very mystery of the Lord among us and not a socio-political empire. That is its overwhelming responsibility.

VII

Toward a New Art of Living

ALPHONSE GOETTMANN: It is believed that more than a million people in Germany meditate regularly every day. Your center is never empty. We meet here people of every age, from all professions, all nationalities. France is also awakening to your teaching. Yet it would seem more interesting to be involved with sports, dance, yoga, rather than sitting in silence in an austere immobility. To what can we attribute this enormous success? Does modern man now feel that he is called to becoming entirely different?

GRAF DÜRCKHEIM: Yes. In the chaos of the moment, man asks himself more than ever about the true meaning of life. But the answer is given only through experience. That is where meditation responds to his desire to realize his complete personhood. The word person comes from *personare*: to ring through, to become an existential self which is transparent to essential Being. The meditative act opens man and allows the divine voice, which is the expression of his essential being, to ring through his conditioned self. From this transparence is born the person, and it is then that man fulfills himself.

AG : This fulfillment becomes a question of life and death in our time. If man is suffocating under pollution, if he finds himself on the eve of a new world war, it is because he is internally asphyxiated and has ceased to be himself. But do you believe that meditation alone will suffice to reconstruct this world that is crumbling?

GD : Everything goes toward man and leaves from man. It is certain that meditation transforms him deeply, but it is only part of a new way of life. It allows one to acquire the "right attitude" which must inhabit us throughout our daily life, for that is the true field of action and exercise. At the beginning of the path we do exercises but, as the experience deepens, we become exercise. It is no longer a knowledge, but a way of being. We reach human maturity when the time in which we lose contact with Being becomes shorter and shorter. According to the old dictum, "each moment is the best of occasions," the practice in daily life means, in all things, recollection and conversion.

Therefore, in awakening to Being within us, we will also feel the essential Being of things and we will encounter Being everywhere in the world.

AG : Is this the meaning of the famous statement by Suzuki which you cited earlier: "Look without as you would look within, making of the without a within"? The exterior becomes a place of inner experience and, little by little, exterior and interior become the expression of the same reality. "Everything has depth" said Paul Tillich, everything is interior.

GD : But this requires other eyes and other ears, and goes beyond an intellectual culture to a culture of inner experience. In other words, we must be freed from our habitual mindset and at the same time be open to a completely new, unexpected path, to a call toward a mission that we had never been conscious of before. We are gifted and capable and created to become witnesses to the reality that we have just experienced. This is a deification which becomes more and more complete. Man learns to listen, to feel the divine through all that he encounters, not only in a beautiful flower or a lovely countryside, but he begins to see the invisible in everything. He hears what cannot be heard. He sees, he feels, he touches the presence; it is therefore through the senses that he begins to bear witness to the divine. For example, he sees in a flower not only the conditioned flower that everyone can see, but he sees through the flower the divine essence in the particular form of that flower. That way of experiencing the life of the flower and of recognizing it is, in turn, a manifestation of the Divine.

Another way of witnessing to the Divine is through action. Whatever we take in hand, literally or figuratively, painting or gardening, building a house or giving form to anything, is again an opportunity. I saw this in Japan, observing a peasant who had to make a hole in a wall. He thought for a long time: "Where will I put this hole, more on the right or the left?" Finally, the place which he found gave the entire wall a particular character which revealed something from beyond: a harmony, which can be found in every piece of art work, otherwise it is not worthy of the name. We speak of art when it is transparent to transcendence; the artist, it goes without saying, is called to manifest the divine in his work, in that which he forms and does. This resonance, the numinous, is for him the primary quality.

The manifestation of the divine in the formation of a person, a person transparent to himself and to others, ought to be the goal of every educator. Take for example a piano teacher: his job is not only to teach students how to play perfectly, but to shape a human being through the apprenticeship of the piano in such a way that the student learns what he must become. Efficiency is not the goal of the work, but rather the becoming of the one who is doing the work. This is the case of one of the great piano masters, Lipati. His worldwide reputation has not kept him from practicing with another great master. For a whole year, he played only Do-Re-Mi. After that, he had acquired the incredible touch that we can appreciate now in listening to his records and concerts. The real touch of the piano is something other than good technique. It is the result of a person who has been transformed.

Finally, a last way to manifest the divine is through love. Love is the true arena of the presence of the divine, but again we must say that love has a completely different quality if we are rooted in transcendence. There is no question here of a sentimental love, the nice, consoling one that reassures and warms, but of a love that recognizes and awakens in the other his or her essential center. That kind of love can be very severe.

Human love in general considers three things: making the other secure, giving meaning to his life and sheltering him in a community. Man is always after this, while love which responds to the call of Being is something entirely different. This is a love that awakens at the core of the beloved a feeling, a warmth there where they find themselves completely lost in meaninglessness and solitude. This is the true shelter. To transmit love from the divine core is to help the other find life in death, meaning beyond meaning and meaninglessness, and love in solitude.

The one who is in contact with Being will therefore be very careful when consoling the beloved. Consolation can be very dangerous. Some time ago, a person wrote to me: "See in what a dead end I find myself; do you have a word of consolation for me?" Knowing this person well, I answered: "Even if I had a word of consolation, I would not give it to you because then I would permit you to remain in your dead end. You must jump out! And if I helped you to put up with your situation, it would be very nice on my part, but a great mistake."

AG : This leap from nice humanism to deification announces

a radical transformation for those who consent to live it. God invites us to a dizzying mutation: to pass from the created to the uncreated, from the human to the divine, from the visible to the invisible, from morality to deification within and through all that we do and undertake. In every moment, we are touched by this "triple radiance" as the liturgy calls it, in a very realistic way: confronted with the dangers of annihilation, diminution and death, the fullness of the Father seeks to engender us. Confronted with the absurdity of life and all the forms of despair, the light of the Son reveals the true meaning of all things. Confronted with solitude and tragedy, love is communicated by the Spirit. When our prayers call for us to become "initiates of the Trinity," they express the very essence of all Christian anthropology, which aims at nothing other than this deification, this transparence of the whole person "in the light of the triple inner sun." We can say that, at each moment, in our attitude, our way of walking and sitting, this human-divine wedding can take place in the simplest way, and is our true vocation outside of which nothing has any meaning. Can you clarify how we are implicated in our totality in this transformation, where daily life is the master?

GD : Nothing exists outside this triple eruption of the great life, incorporated into all that exists. Our work is to be open and to stay in contact with it. The openness of inner consciousness begins through a way of being here as the body that we are. It is a presence that senses immediately when it has lost the golden thread that unites us with the essential. It is an attitude of constant seeking, like the hunting dog who never loses the trace of the game. Attention is always directed toward the depths. In Japan, a friend asked me if I did the exercise of zazen. I replied: "Yes," and he asked me: "When?"

"In the morning from seven to eight o'clock."

"Oh. So you have not yet understood anything. If you do not continue it all day long, it won't do you any good."

But if I had said: "I am in exercise all day long," he would have said: "That does you no good if you don't do a particular exercise in the morning." So the two go together to put man in a state of continual awakening. Meditation acts on our way of being in daily life, and daily life acts on meditation but, in both cases, it is the same attitude. Whatever we do: walking, sitting, peeling potatoes, knitting or the most superficial thing, we can look within and remain open to the possibility of being touched by the divine. No situation of existential life should be closed off—we are to be watchful all the time. Only right attitude allows us to advance and mature on this path; it is impossible if you are tensed, shoulders contracted and lifted up, stomach held in and breathing on the surface, uncentered. All these behaviors are expressions on the outside of what you are within: dominated by a little arrogant, anguished and solitary self. It is a prison whose doors are locked. As long as the little self has not blown open the doors and left its cell, no contact with Being is possible. Consider all those so-called religious persons whose apparent sainthood is only an enormous cramp! Their features are strained, their lips tight, their gaze distracted, their faces without joy.

AG : These last few centuries of self-made spirituality have often introduced a subtle pride into the search for interiority, which has made the demons descend into the street, if not into the convents and religious communities, where people often tear each other apart.

GD : Man is an inseparable whole. If he is divided in himself, the body on one side, the soul on the other and the spirit who knows where, what can he bring to others, what can he radiate around him, except his desperate state?

AG : Is not right attitude in the unity body-soul-spirit easier for a person who works with their hands than for an intellectual whose mind is always occupied?

GD : We have to differentiate between the intellectual worker using what is necessary and useful from his mind, and the rationalist who identifies himself completely with his reason. I believe that fundamentally, for true mathematicians or physicians there is a great spiritual or religious surge that can accompany them throughout their work, and the discovery of the solution to a problem can be a very intense moment of spiritual experience. Their career is their way of responding to that longing for the extraordinary mystery of life and their entering into the essential. It is an extremely pious attitude, and is perfectly possible at the heart of the laboratory.

AG : The theory of relativity was discovered by Einstein during an absolutely fabulous spiritual experience, a dazzling eruption of Being. The rational verification came only afterward and it is far from being finished. Will it ever be? Because to really understand, one would have to undergo the same experience instead of merely thinking about the concept. There is the cramp of mathematicians just as there is the cramp of sainthood. But let's consider schools. What kind of a person is being formed there?

GD : The problem is widespread. As soon as we have another vision of the human being, we can see to what extent he is mutilated everywhere. It must be said that education today is particularly disastrous. Take the domain of sports: it is only a poor caricature of what it could be. During a conference of athletes, I said: "Ladies and gentlemen, you have doubtless run a four–hundred meter race in your lifetime. When it was successful, did you not experience that it was no longer you who were running, but another through you?" There was a great silence. After the conference, one of the athletes came toward me: "You have said something extraordinary. After an illness, I started running again; to my amazement, I ran the fastest race of my life, and it was not me but another. I experienced then a feeling of great depth, of divine beauty, a joy as I have never again tasted in my life. And now, thanks to what you have said, I understand that that moment was not only the summit of my life as an athlete, but could have been the beginning of a new life. I should have understood that it was an experience of Being that required another kind of work made possible because of this transformation in myself. My exercises should have been done from that point of view to remain in contact with the essential Reality that I had just discovered."

It is this kind of personal discovery that makes us understand the decay of modern sports. The rule of the Olympic Games is a terrible thing.

AG : Performance, classification and politics have replaced the mystical attitude of ancient times. The famous catharsis which the Greeks experienced both in the games as well as in the theaters provoked a divine explosion in the actor and in the spectator. Perhaps there remains a little of this in the shouting of the crowds in the stadiums. I don't believe it is simply collective psychosis. *En–theos*, the root of enthusiasm, means in Greek: to be in God. In ancient times, Greek education created liturgical beings: their games, along with their music and art, were of great importance in the schools. It was the practice of worship. We still find today this same veneration in Japanese archery, as you have experienced.

GD : Yes. When I lived in Japan I was at the same school as Herrigel, the author of *Zen in the Art of Archery*. For three years we learned how to shoot on a straw target one meter in diameter at three meters in distance. It was not a matter of hitting the target, but of developing an ensemble of movements that were the condition for a technique of true archery. The goal is that one day, after years of exercise, you can perfectly master the technique in such a way that you shoot without the intervention of the self, and to the total exclusion of the will. When the ambition to hit the target and the fear of missing it are completely removed, then the technique, absolutely cleansed of all ambition and know-how and liberated from the little self, makes possible in and through your depths the release of the arrow. It is no longer you who shoot, but the deep reality which shoots through you and, in a particular act, sings the eternal song of the apparition of Being. At that moment, the one who shoots has the extraordinary experience of something amazing that passes through him. The spectators who have "eyes to see" perceive prodigious radiance emanating from the one who shoots.

There is also the tea ceremony in Japanese tradition; everything is in the preparation. But to prepare the tea, up to the moment when it is sipped, requires a certain number of movements. We learn to execute each movement with perfection and then tie them all together. Done in the attitudes we have spoken of, this offers, not only to the one who sees it but also to the one who lives it, the possibility of a contact with Transcendence.

AG : This is undoubtedly a rare lesson in the spiritual value of apprenticeship in the simple movements of daily life.

GD : Certainly. If, with the same seriousness, you make gestures in daily life that are repeated over and over, then you will one day be able to make these gestures without the self getting involved, and you will be able to have the same experience. Everything can become exercise. My master Teramoto told me that his principle exercise in the morning was to shave—that there was a sequence of movements, which were the same each day, and that in seeking to perfect them, he was offering himself the opportunity for a profound experience.

We only see something where we look for it, and we only find something where we are searching. At all times, in every circumstance, we can develop our inner consciousness, awaken the taste of the numinous. An action as simple as walking can be an excellent medium for learning openness to Being; nothing but conscious walking. That is, by the way, a highly esteemed exercise in Japan: the *Kin–hin*. It is a matter of feeling the act, not to think it, but to do it in full consciousness, with the attention directed toward our depth. That is why, among our automatic movements, breathing is such a privileged area. As soon as you follow it consciously, without interference, you can be seized by the divine breath.

This can be applied to any job. For instance, an accountant who adds numbers all day long. His way of being there while writing those numbers can be a prayer. The fact that his consciousness is occupied by some work does not in any way inhibit contact with Being. The issue is to always know how this particular work that I am doing allows me to train myself in the right attitude to witness to the divine. Look at a bricklayer; the way in which he throws the cement on the wall. What a magnificent movement, it's like a dance. For the master mason, there can be a numinous experience in the repetition of this gesture. Or painters who always make the same movement. I know several for whom it is a true spiritual exercise. The farmer, when he uses his hoe, can make of it a religious act. Look at his face. And the craftsmen: the shoemaker, the metal worker. In the workshops where they have worked for ten or twenty years, where they always make the same movements, there is a numinous quality in the atmosphere that opens up your senses as soon as you come in contact with it.

AG : Unfortunately, there are also all the jobs that are less in continuity and harmony with human nature. I think of the worker crushed by assembly line work, those I have seen work in thousand–degree heat near the great furnaces, or kneeling four hundred meters under ground in the night of the coal mines. I have rarely entered into an experience of the mystery of life as powerful as the contact with these terrified faces, disfigured and yet transfigured by a look that plunged me into my depths. But are they conscious of being witnesses of the light?

GD : Their situation is comparable to that of soldiers on the front, facing danger and death. To the extent that they accept the unacceptable, they may be invaded by a feeling of profound liberation, at the very heart of their slavery. In any case, nothing, not even their atrocious conditions can inhibit their advance on the inner path.

AG : On the contrary, it may be difficult to admit but it seems to me that the more prestige and the more things of this world that are refused to them, the more they are open to the other world present in their depths. That explains why Jesus called them "blessed" and the first elect of His kingdom. That also explains why they can, when they want to, put this enormous force within them in the service of workers' solidarity and the struggle for justice.

VIII

Shadows and Lights on the Way

ALPHONSE GOETTMANN: Several thousand years ago Patanjali, the father of Yoga, said: "Practice is the intensity of permanent vigilance." In other words, whether it is meditation or daily life as exercise, everything depends on attention; it is the fundamental attitude and the key to awakening to the divine. All religious traditions are unanimous on this subject. But how do we make this conviction a reality? That is the real problem. How do we maintain a sustained and uninterrupted attention in a world which is ingenious at endlessly distracting it and dividing us? Don't our good intentions risk remaining dead words?

GRAF DÜRCKHEIM: Of course. Permanent attention is the first art that we must exercise. It is a state of critical awareness that constantly watches the movements of our spirit and of our body. This is very difficult. Attention contains the word tension: it is a "tension toward" something, without contraction, animated by the yearning for a faithful contact with Being. In a recent article, Doctor Stachel points out what zazen brings to Christians and admits that he himself had learned through it how to pray the Our

Father without distraction. But what does it mean "to be distracted"? One day I asked Guardini what he thought of a child who yawned during the Our Father. He answered that it must not be allowed.

"And why not?" I responded, "There is nothing more normal and it still happens to me today."

"But that is distraction."

"To yawn when we say 'forgive us our sins' means that we effectively realize the prayer, because forgiveness has provoked a letting go and a relaxation within us and something new can begin."

AG : Recollection and prayer, as with work, especially intellectual work, are practically impossible without relaxation. Through muscular relaxation, the person comes out of his strangle-hold and has access to recollection with much more ease. But in which novitiate or school is this taught?

GD : Once the condition of relaxation is achieved, we educate the attention through concentration on an object, and we try to remain with it for a time. In all ages and in all traditions, the object that works best is breathing. By consciously following our breathing, we are able to eliminate all thoughts that arise "like a horde of monkeys around your head," according to a Japanese saying. They go away only if you are able to remain concentrated on a single point.

AG : Are we not touching upon the secret of all geniuses, and especially of the saints? The biographers of Francis of Assisi said that he concentrated a gigantic energy on a single point. Swami Sivananda speaks so much of the "one pointed mind," of the spirit concentrated on a single object. In the same way, the ancient tradition of the Prayer of Jesus focuses the whole being on a single center—the heart.

GD : I have personal experience of the profound efficacy of the Jesus Prayer. It is the Christian *mantra* par excellence. *The Way of the Pilgrim*, which tells of this practice, greatly interested me. It makes reference to a book known as *The Philokalia*, and on that subject a strange thing happened to me. I was very intrigued and asked myself whether this *Philokalia* existed or whether it was an invention of the Russian pilgrim. And the very minute that I was reflecting on this, a postman knocked at my door and gave me a card from a Russian lady living in Paris. I did not know her at all and yet she wrote: "Sir, in reading one of your books, I had the impression that the *Philokalia* might interest you. I want to inform you that there is now an English translation of the original." Eight days later I had the *Philokalia* in my hands, and I could read the commentaries of the Fathers of the Church on the Prayer of Jesus.

AG : For once the "small voice" made itself external.

GD : God's voice, not mine.

Dürckheim with Goettmann

AG : Father Lassalle, one of the finest Western specialists in Zen, said that the Prayer of Jesus is the closest thing to Zen meditation in the Christian tradition. According to his own experience, breathing plays an important role, as does the exclusion of all discursive thought in order to find the heart as the unifying center.

GD : I know Father Lassalle very well. It is with him that I introduced zazen in Germany during a session of four hundred participants on the theme: "East–West." He has nearly half a century of zazen practice behind him, he has written big books on the subject, and he is certain that, through the exercise of zazen, the openness to Christ becomes greater and greater.

AG : The exercise of zazen is certainly a very great school of attention. Nothing makes you more present to the passing second than sitting in total immobility while being conscious of the mysterious activity of life; attention is then at its peak.

GD : The problem of attention is nevertheless more difficult during the day; it doesn't just happen by itself. Permanent vigilance is the fruit of a definitive decision of the individual. It presupposes a decision that comes from the core of your being as it progresses on the way. The depth of the decision is the only assurance of loyalty to the path that you want to take. It is only when you have truly decided to climb to the summit of a mountain that you will not turn back at the first sign of fatigue. The depth of the commitment is the best assurance of attention. Beyond the promise of entering on the way, or of remaining in a certain attitude for a period of time, it is a decision that gives us a bad conscience at every infidelity, along with a feeling of betrayal.

Loyalty to exercises requires the same conditions. In the firmness of the decision is found the point of honor in relation to God: if we let go, we betray ourselves and the inner master who is more severe than the external master. It is also a question of discipline:

outside of discipline imposed by the exterior, there is the one which is interior to us, and which we take in full freedom. It is very different from the outer one because it becomes flesh within us and allows us to achieve a decision that might seem useless or ridiculous at certain moments.

AG : Good relaxation, concentration on a single point, and a decision lived in a stern discipline are therefore the levers of attention. It seems to me that the consciousness of living a decisive choice requires that everything become organized around this primary goal. Beyond confused or contradictory aspirations, the requirement of the decision forces us to select, to place priorities in values and initiatives, to painfully eliminate other things. We then enter into a state of offering: is this not the meaning of sacrifice? In the eyes of some people, we diminish ourselves per-haps, or divide ourselves, while in reality the true decision centers us completely, regroups and unifies us. We live intensely from the present and forge the future.

GD : This is a true asceticism, and without asceticism there is no progress. As Saint Thomas said, "Asceticism is a well–ordered work whose result is a constitution of man that expresses the fullness of Being." What a definition! That's it, and even if few people achieve it, this path leads to the presence. The person who has experienced it has no more doubts, but is always in danger of falling back into a false and ungrateful attitude to this recognition. We never achieve perfection and no one can pretend to have attained the state of perpetual vigilance. "The righteous fall seven times a day," says the Bible.

AG : That is where the "reminders" at regular times are very helpful.

GD : Each person should have an object at home, even if it is a little stone which reminds him of the wholly other. For many, it is a cross, an image; for me, it is the face of Christ, the Holy Shroud of Turin, always there, facing my work table and reminding me of who I am.

AG : In every Orthodox home there is a little iconostasis, the icon corner, before which a candle burns permanently. But a candle burns in your home as well.

GD : Yes. The lit candle is part of the space where I work. It is for me a sign of light and of life, as is incense.

We can also carry in our pockets a chestnut or any kind of object: at their simple contact we return to the right attitude. There is nothing magical in this, the objects themselves have no importance. It is what they say to us that counts, it is the call they represent that is important. Finally, what can help us a great deal in daily life is ritual. Unfortunately, when I ask my students what their ritual is, I notice with sadness that many of them do not have any. But those who adopt one are very happy with the experience. This is an ensemble of signs that we give ourselves to express the link between existence and the divine. Each person can find his proper ceremonial: for example, at the beginning and end of a day offering a prayer either standing or on one's knees, prostrating oneself, making the sign of the cross, raising our hands in offering. This puts us back on the path toward God.

AG : And the more the gesture is pure and free from the control of the self, the more man becomes transparent. But from the pure gesture to pure consciousness there is a long road to travel.

GD : What blocks it is what depth psychology calls the "shadow"; it is something dark in man, and therefore dangerous, because he runs away from it and identifies himself with his facade, which he wants to maintain and which he believes to be part of his primitive consciousness: "Yes, I am good, I am honest, etc." This education to "do good; behave as we should; be in harmony with the ethics of a community," all this permits man to forget what there really is behind the facade. Behind it is the shadow, the vital impulses that should have been part of the life he lives, but whose expression has been inhibited. The wholeness of the person has not been able to blossom: his first movements have been withheld, his desires and impulses constantly repressed or eliminated, his creativity often stifled, natural expressions, aggressions or needs suffocated, even the call toward beautiful things has been restricted. These taboos and obstacles are as varied as individuals, but the desire that always returns to most people is the one of getting rid of the imprint of their parents and the authorities of their childhood. In my subconscious, I would have liked to kill my father. Not only did I not do it, but I never even resisted him when he yelled at me. I always took everything from my father and mother because I was a good boy, according to the usual conviction, "the good boy is the one who obeys." What a terrible statement! "Children are good because they obey." This authoritarianism is at the center of many human malformations. It is the father who says of his children, "I don't know what they want. They always speak of their freedom. In my house, everyone must do what I want." This desire to kill, not our father or our mother, but the image that we have of them within us, is generally widespread: each person must recognize it and take it out of himself, otherwise there is no valid becoming on the path. This image is also the origin of all our aggressions against God.

AG : Once the relationship with our parents is solved, the question still remains, "What is playing for me today the enveloping role of the falsely protective mother or father?" Almost as soon as the umbilical cord has been cut, we have built a warm nest someplace else: family, community, Church, or a simple friendship, even the comforts of one's home or car, everything can become subject to a very ambiguous relationship and inhibit man from being himself.

GD : The subconscious is more and more poisoned and finally all nature is disturbed. Certainly it is not just the parents with all their taboos who are the source of this shadow. School education and society, bureaucracies, take over after childhood; each individual enforces upon himself his behavior, his ethic, his appearance.

AG : White on the exterior, black on the interior. A little like those many churches in Rome: some of them are masterpieces, but many have only a marvelous facade that hides a terrible house behind them. Man seeks to save face and hides the essential.

GD : The deepest shadow is at the same time the repressed primordial light, the denial of essential Being in human consciousness. This is our intrinsic evil. Nothing interferes with the development of man more than that permanent source of discontent, inexplicable suffering, and physical and psychological illnesses. We must become conscious of this repression of essential Being and, instead of suffocating it, we must awaken to it. Then, thanks to its manifestation, we will allow life to enlarge the horizon of the experience into supra-worldly dimensions.

AG : Can this shadow which filters everything and makes us live in a continual lie in relation to ourselves, far from our deep reality, heal itself through meditation alone, or are other therapies also needed?

GD : It is a long work to discern and integrate the powerful energies of the shadow. But the person who has become conscious of the oppression of his essential Being, and has decided at all costs to undertake the hard exercises of a regular meditation, enters into a process of transformation and can advance on the path of initiation until full light is reached. Unfortunately, the Holy Spirit cannot always erase a father complex. Everything depends on our way of praying or meditating and the intimate consciousness of the immanent Christ within us as a living experience. It is only at this contact that the emancipation of man can take place and the true life open its eyes. But this often requires other means than meditation. One of my collaborators has just returned from a monastery where she practiced psychodrama with seven sisters. She was deeply touched to see one of them suddenly spill out all that she had been hiding behind her nun's clothing for some twenty years. Another no longer knew how to pray. There we can see the facade of beings who behave well but who are very far from their reality. It is incredible to find how much our unconscious is withholding. We must become conscious of these dark forces, take them seriously and accept them. Outside of psychodrama, there are many other possibilities: depth psychology, psychotherapy, group therapy, gestal therapy, and many other current ways of releasing all that. But here again, discernment is crucial. Too often what is offered today does not take the whole person into account; we tear down walls built around the instincts, we liberate the subconscious, and finally, we are so stripped that we lose our own mystery.

AG : That is where those incomprehensible suicides after years of analysis come from. A therapy that does not take into account the spiritual dimension of human beings is doomed to failure. Christ himself said to the sick: "Come to me. I will give you rest." He continues to say this today through the liturgy and the sacraments, those signs of His presence among us. We have witnessed a number of healings.

GD : To the extent that participation in liturgy involves the whole person, that the little self is left outside, that you are ready to give yourself completely, to submit yourself authentically to the One who is above you, then you can go very far into your depth.

You become humble, that is, capable of letting go not only of an exterior facade, but the will to have, to know, and also many inner things: attitudes which are at the foundations of the shadow. I am sure that a deeply religious being is aware of all that lies hidden behind his facade and, under the impulse of Being, many knots are undone. True religiosity is certainly the best tool for cleaning the subconscious.

But it is important to go beyond the ethical level and discover the source of that evil. Otherwise your charity would run the risk of being only an escape and the expression of the shadow.

The Orthodox liturgy certainly offers an experience of awakening and the transformation of being. But let us not forget that an experience of awakening does not create an awakened person. The door is opened toward the mystery within. You are on the path of initiation, but it is a beginning, not an end.

Most liturgies today have dried up in a flood of abstract words and an almost total absence of gestures. The first person responsible for this is the priest or the worship leader. In the past, movements occurred in the choir and it was important that the priest live the ceremony in the smallest gesture and to the ends of his fingertips, like a sacred dance coming from his contact with inner transcendence. The words and gestures in themselves, cut off from all the rest, do not go very far. If the celebrants understood that every liturgy can transform even their bodies and give a form to their transparence, then the faithful would be opened to mystery and transformed in turn. The priests would rediscover their true role as servants of the divine in man. I know that the power of the sacraments is not dependent on this, but those who want to have that experience would be all the more deeply touched.

AG : All that you say concerns me deeply, and I am conscious of my responsibility, because I too was one of those priests who celebrated masses stripped of everything, without gestures or ornaments, in near immobility. When I was initiated to celebrate the Holy Mysteries as an Orthodox priest, I submitted myself for weeks and still do today to the rigors of the exercises of relaxation, breathing, right attitude and pure gesture, the tone of voice and the training for singing. It is not simply a matter of mastering a ritual, but of entering into an anthropological totality to which the Church as Body of Christ and Fullness of Spirit invites us, whether it be in liturgy, in theology, or in the Christian life.

IX

Commitment:
Cross of Christ or Red Cross?

ALPHONSE GOETTMANN: We have been moving along the path of initiation for a good while now, but aren't we giving the impression of going it alone? What becomes of others, humanity, the world, while we occupy ourselves with the inner life? Faced with militants, soldiers, strikers, with all those who will go as far as giving their lives for a more just world, don't we seem like "navel gazers?"

GRAF DÜRCKHEIM: There was once a Japanese master who regularly made the rounds of his monastery. One day, he encountered the cook who said to him: "Master, I am a communist, so I think about others, and when I do the cooking, I think of our monks to make good food for them." He gathered his courage and asked:

"Master, about whom and about what do you think all day long?"

"Oh," answered the master, "I only think about myself."

The cook was frightened. What does it mean to say "I think about myself all day"?

The question is often asked: "Don't the people who meditate and take the inner way become egoists?" This is a great misunderstanding, for we are not digging into our existential self, but are seeking to be anchored in Being. This requires, as we have stated, an indispensable work on our subconscious and on ourselves. We take care of ourselves, but for what purpose? Precisely to open ourselves to the transcendent reality at the heart of the self that, by definition, is universal love!

Quite often, we notice in persons who are so–called "social activists" a flattery of the little self, or an escape from the essential in whose name they have become involved in the first place. The great scandal of the "do–gooders" and of the pharisees is precisely this shadow with which the mundane self obscures the Christ within them: then He is the suffocated life, the rejected way, the unrecognized truth.

AG : What do we then bring to others, if not our own misery?

GD : Work on oneself and meditation are exactly the opposite of "navel gazing"; they explode the sick egocentrism and liberate the light. Is it not for this light above all that people yearn? "My kingdom is not of this world," said the Christ, but "it is in you."

AG : "They are in the world, but not of it."

GD : And He recognizes us as "brothers" and we are called to follow him. But the one who has not experienced His presence within knows nothing of this brotherhood, nor of the way to follow. His involvement remains "of the world" and does not deal with real needs. We must not confuse the cross of Christ with the "Red Cross" and Christianity with social militancy. Certainly, the Red Cross is an important branch on the tree of Christ, but it is not the tree itself. Only the contact with our deepest interiority and the birth of the new man within can radically change us in relation to the world and others. It is only at this level that the

other can be perceived as a companion on the way, in a consciousness that we are one in Being. Life is no longer the same and the
vision of the world has nothing in common with the old ways of
seeing things: we then begin to see the meaning of mission and
commitment from an entirely different point of view. Putting
aside all that is agitation on the surface, questioning even certain
friendly or communal ties, we may seem bizarre, disloyal or ab-
normal in the eyes of many, but it doesn't matter because we are
in other dimensions and no longer have the same points of reference.

AG : The man who restored Western Orthodoxy, Monseigneur
Jean de Saint-Denis, had extraordinary words to say on this subject. The initial act of all effort, he stated, is to become a person,
to become conscious of one's place before God and what He wants
from us.

"Our attention must be projected like an arrow toward the
center: the Christ. True human community is comparable to a
circle formed by brothers and sisters holding hands, carrying each
other's burdens, but their gaze is focused on the center: the Christ.
Our greatness comes from our answer to the love of God for us."

GD : God calls man from the beginning: "Adam, where are
you?" Only those whose inner ear has opened know that man does
not really become man unless he answers this call, which resonates
ceaselessly and should always follow us. Relationships with others
can only reach their fullness there, where we have discovered their
true meaning. To love is to awaken in the other a supra–worldly
dimension and become free for service to Being. To love one's
neighbor is to help him discover the three fundamental impulses
of life: its vital source, its meaning and its unity.

This is exactly what we seek in meditation, face to face with
God. I often say: "A good meditation produces three effects: you
feel strong even if you are weak, for it is another force, different

from natural strength or weakness; you are in order internally even if everything is in disorder; and you especially find yourself in contact with unity.

You will have the feeling that the trees bow as you go by, that the stones smile, the grass moves to greet you and the people who walk by will feel closer to you than ever before. Yet your kindness and your goodness will have nothing to do with ethics. The quality of love which is an expression of Being is not the result of a submission of egoism to an ethical behavior but to the values of the good, the beautiful, the real.

AG : We do not incorporate ourselves into the standard morals, but into the triple force of the divine Trinity.

GD : On this level, goodness and beauty have nothing to do with ethics or aestheticism. They are the expression of the presence of the divine, which manifests itself under these three aspects, but it is the great third one, the unity of all, which takes hold of you and integrates you into the movement of divine Life, in such a way that you cannot do otherwise than be what others would call "good or beautiful."

We must learn to differentiate between the attitude that is an expression of Being, and the attitude that is a submission to the ethical law. There is no need to make efforts for that which comes from the heart; if we must force ourselves to be good, it is no longer an emanation of Being. We are no longer in the domain of the will.

AG : "Thy will be done." We enter into absolute conscience, unbearable for all institutions that live from ethics and morals.

GD : Such a consciousness is always revolutionary because it goes beyond the framework of a community. But that doesn't mean that we are free to do anything we please, for we do not live according to the whims of our desires and we will constantly have to submit our egos to human requirements.

Dürckheim on a visit to the Goettmanns

AG : This is putting ourselves in the hands of God, even at the risk of being judged by those around you: "He saved others, but he cannot save himself," someone said as an insult to Christ on the cross. But that is the price of love—it seeks neither to flatter nor to please others.

GD : This leads to the whole issue of humility. There are two kinds of humility: on the ethical level, someone will say: "Don't pretend to be more than what you are, don't inflate yourself." On the level of absolute conscience, humility is much heavier to carry:

it is first a matter of becoming conscious, of recognizing the graces and gifts received, of not using them for personal power, but at the same time putting them in service to others by witnessing to the divine. Don't pretend to be more or less than you are. Before God we are all the same size, but among men, we are all on different stages along the path. It is a privileged person who is conscious of witnessing to the divine. Indeed, "many are called, but few are chosen." Yes, we are chosen, and we must not be afraid to admit it, because that is what we are, as part of a very specific mission.

AG : The "elect" have heard the call and seek to answer it. They form the "little remnant" or the "little flock" of which the Bible speaks. They are not superior to others, but must be the leaven in the bread, the light on the way, so that all may advance and ascend. Isn't that the true involvement with the poor and the deprived?

GD : That is not easy to answer. Are these the poor in the material, cultural or spiritual sense? There are those who are rich with intellectual gifts and yet who are absolutely poor and deaf to the message. Often in my conferences, well educated people leave because they do not understand a single word but, at the door, laborers wait for me to say; "We do not understand your language, but we appreciate what you are saying." On the level of inner knowledge, the distinction between poor and rich does not mean anything.

As for the social level, it would be absolutely ridiculous to believe that the one who is on the inner path no longer needs to be responsible for others and especially for the poor. But it is not a matter of bringing them opium as was done for centuries and saying: "Resign yourselves, your suffering will be rewarded, what could be better than going hungry?" Meditation does not feed empty stomachs, but it opens us to another source which is beyond ethical goodness.

AG : The poor must find their human dignity and not be used to ease the consciences of the do–gooders. "Man does not live by bread alone," and if we give him only one or the other, the material or the spiritual, he will never be a man.

GD : It is said that in France Marxism is interesting the clergy more and more. Because Christ supposedly wanted to remake the world, Marx becomes a Christian commodity: "He understood the poor." What a confusion of levels. Christ never worked for "having" but for "Being." The movement of the worker–priests is another matter for, instead of preaching, they seek to live with others and witness through their way of living. I recently had a visit from a missionary to Katanga; after twenty years in mission, he asked himself what he had accomplished, if he had only spent his time serving the institution and indoctrinating the natives. He now wants to leave his nice parsonage, live in community with the natives, and "be" rather than speak.

There are many who build on sand, and their convictions are founded on a misunderstanding. I often hear sermons on the radio and I sometimes have the impression that the preachers, in presenting God as a superhuman, are working for the Adversary. If God is a superhuman, injustice as it is in the world is unacceptable and faith is shaken by disgust. This comes out of a judgement from the existential self. And we seek justice through an external consolation of our human distresses. You see the confusion. Faith finds its justifications in completely different reasons.

AG : Why didn't Jesus Christ become political?

GD : Because through the political disaster of the time there was an opportunity to witness to that which was beyond all politics. If he had tried to develop, even with great intelligence, the idea of a reform of the state of Israel, it might have lasted thirty years, and then what? The message of Christ is valid for every situation and for all times; it deals with all the distresses of life. In a beautiful book Simone de Beauvoir tells of a man who had made a pact with the Devil in order not to die. He becomes an adviser to a state and for fifty years builds fortresses which would last forever. Then he travels to another country. When he comes back a hundred years later, no one remembers the problems he thought he had forever resolved. All that seems important to us today is forgotten tomorrow. What is left of revolutions and wars other than monuments to the dead? The message of Christ brings life. It reveals that which is beyond the ephemeral and the transitory, and goes beyond the usual horizon and all that occupies us in the moment: it is a call to an attitude of eternity. The true combat is on another level, and deals with the deification of man and not only with the agreeable conditions of life. Because of that, the message of Christ cannot age, it is always new. In the same way, the wisdom of Lao–Tzu cannot disappear. True wisdom is always universal and cannot be expressed in human language because it is an expression of Being.

AG : The under–development of man, the radical rupture in his being, and his inner anguish are the common denominators of all the different forms of under–development: psychological, physiological and material misery, in the East as in the West. The pain is ontological. What man needs most of all today is to adore. From this perspective, when action or commitment is grounded in the inner source of Being, there is a lasting effect. It means placing oneself on the only level where the breakthroughs in history occur. Today we need a kind of active wisdom that links the inner and the outer, that realizes that the inner and the outer are two poles of an inseparable whole, a wisdom that is both a liberation of the extraordinary potential of the spiritual forces in human beings and an instrument of combat for justice. For the person who meditates, another world is possible because another man is possible in the very structure of his being, and he verifies that every day in the most concrete experiences. We have here the unseen role that meditation has played in the lives of all the great spiritual persons of history. They have good reason to believe that the radical modification of humanity, and the future of the world, depend on spiritual experience.

X

"Teacher, Where Do You Live?"
(John 1:38)

GRAF DÜRCKHEIM: For centuries there was an uninterrupted thread from Jesus Christ to the great saints whom you have mentioned. They were luminous beacons on the paths of wisdom. Today, these paths sink into darkness for lack of light: there are no more guides. Human beings are victims of the dehumanizing universe of technology, where efficiency and production are primary. But man's rebellion is opening a new age. There are many who have discovered within them the yearning for another reality and feel imperatively the call of the master. But which master? The attraction to India and the guru reflect the rejection of masters from our modern societies, whose wisdom is summarized in ideologies and power. Man's desire is elsewhere, his distress has led him into an impasse, and only the spiritual master can answer his cry. The master is the archetype toward which man aspires: the way to have access to inner experience and realize the whole dimension of his life.

The two pillars on which the existence of a Western believer rests are the organization of this world and the faith in another. This leaves completely fallow the spiritual maturity of man and his ability to experience that which he only believes piously. The enormous consequence is that quite often those who have the levers of command in the world and in the Church are incredibly immature; the very organ that would allow them to feel this gap fails them completely. They are then outside of reality. In such confusion, the need for spiritual masters becomes more urgent than ever. Will they appear?

ALPHONSE GOETTMANN: And how to recognize them? Because the false prophets are already here, merchants in the temple and other charlatans as well. Many improvise the role of "Master" and make a business out of it. Seekers want powers, horoscopes, artificial paradises and many recipes for inner happiness. I have never met so many people who wander from one group to another and end up healing their indigestion with psychiatrists.

GD: "When the student is ready, the master appears," is a current saying. Those whom you mention have not yet touched the true level of human despair, they are not yet on the way; perhaps they are on the way toward the way, but as long as they do not feel attracted by the unique reality, they risk going astray into satanic nets. The false masters assume majestic gestures which have no inner truth. They often impress others with miracles which only occur on the existential level. They use magic that effects extraordinary changes without transformation. They develop an arrogance in the disciple who then believes himself to be better than others. They answer the ambitions of the existential self in their clients. What they do can be seen and reveals their lies. Instead of feeding the true, which is expressed in humility, they satisfy the thirst for extraordinary experiences and superior powers.

The authentic seeker is no longer fooled: in his inner silence, he perceives the voice of the master who inhabits him and recognizes in his depths the one who approaches him. The inner master and the exterior master are founded on a third: the eternal master. The three are the manifestation of the supernatural life in a natural, human form. Only the one who unconditionally enters the way is a true student or disciple. Master-disciple-way are three inseparable givens.

By eternal master, I mean the principle, the original image or the archetype of universal man; it is the *homo maximus* in which Being is realized, life in the totality of its three aspects: fullness, order and unity, in a particular form always in process of trans-formation. The eternal master lifts the veil from his presence when man comes to the extreme limits of conscious or unconscious resistance to the life within him; when through illness, depression, unexpected circumstances and surprising "coincidences," man hears the voice of his asphyxiated Being; but also when he becomes more sensitive to his yearning for liberation, to the more frequent touches of the numinous and finally to experiences of Being, small or great. Then little by little, or in one mighty blow, the old world crumbles, a new consciousness is born, and with it the eternal master takes the shape of the inner master.

Only this awakening to the inner master allows man to en-counter and recognize the exterior master, for the one he seeks has already been found. He becomes at the same time the inner disciple who opens himself to the inner way, and only then are the conditions set for an encounter with the exterior master. The master is not actually someone exterior, but the mirror of our own depth. The master whom we meet on the outside is the one whom we are within. He incarnates and fully accomplishes that to which we only aspire. The master has crossed over many stages that are still hidden to us, he represents the fullness of life that we have hardly awakened to, the true and only maturity of man in his total liberty. Nothing chains him down, his thought and action are no longer dominated by social, moral and theological prerogatives. If he respects the order of this world, he is not submitted to it. On the contrary, when some "order" keeps life from realizing itself within and around him, he overthrows, destroys, dissolves and breaks all that obstructs the way. The master is then dangerous and harsh for those who seek an easy peace, security and harmony. As with life, he is always new, revolutionary, unexpected and contradictory, always creative and never rigid, because the important thing is to advance, to be transformed and to die in order to live. For the disciple, this signifies the end of all false peace, the annunciation of a combat to the death for a life that is beyond all peace and all trouble, beyond all life or death.

But the master never acts of himself, his source is a higher impulse, and his humility is perfect. He lives in reference to God or to his own master, and feels responsible before him for his mission. His values are not the beautiful, the true and the good, but love.

AG : The divine teaching is always the same. When the prophet Jeremiah was invested with his mission in the Old Testament, God said to him; "I establish you in this day over the nations and the kingdoms, to tear down... build and plant!" And Jesus, the ultimate master, said: "I did not come to bring peace but a sword." It is indeed a statement that we are not used to hearing among so-called "spiritual masters." But the joy of the disciple is measured by the price that he is willing to pay. "Blessed are those who are persecuted for righteousness' sake, for theirs is the kingdom of heaven."

GD : No one is a disciple without being marked by fire with the seal of "All or nothing." To be awake is one thing, to hear the call and follow the master on the way is something else. In the first instance, we have the possibility of becoming a disciple, in the second we are one: what now distinguishes the disciple from the

Dürckheim late in life

master is nothing else but the distance that separates them, but they are on the same path. In other words, the disciple has accepted the harsh discipline and the loyalty to a decision with no turning back. Then it is not he who has taken the way, but it is the way that has taken him. "You have not chosen me, I have chosen you," said Christ. At this stage, the advance is irreversible, whatever the temptations or hesitations, and the risks of falling back become more and more rare, while the process of transformation and transparence deepens continually.

AG : What are the means by which the master forms the "inner man" of the disciple?

GD : Among the varied gifts of the Spirit, we can especially recognize five that seem essential for the master: teaching, practical direction, radiance, example and shock.

The core of the master's teaching cannot be put into formulas or explained. It is heart–to–heart, a matter of relationship, not of thought. The experience of transcendence will always remain ineffable. We can approach it through reflection, discover the preliminaries and the consequences, the meaning and movement of the way; but that is all, and that is not what is important. The master has only one thing to communicate, always the same thing, and he does it in a thousand and one ways, letting its countless facets, colors and lights scintillate very simply through his way of being here. However old his tradition may be, he reconstitutes it in his own way, as it takes life and shape within him. The essential is never what the master says, but how he says it. The spark does not erupt from statements, but from the Being of the one who makes them, and because he has achieved what he is speaking about. That is why the master has no pedagogical behavior. He does not seek to analyze, to instruct, or to give advice. His only goal is to place his disciple under the call of the essential so that he might feel it and love it from his own depths.

The goal of practical direction is to shake the tyranny of the little self and to liberate Being. The master sometimes tries the confidence of the disciple through very harsh trials by asking him to do something that he dislikes or which he does not understand. Yet obedience must be total and absolute, not out of respect for some authority or external rule, but because the master and disciple are seeking the same and only reality. An order from the master, however hard and severe it may be, is always charged with fullness of life that is only the expression of the love that ties him to the disciple in the unity of Being. He follows him step by step in the exercises and accompanies him intimately in his transformation, correcting his attitude, and sometimes abruptly intervening. The exercises often go to the limit of the bearable to force the self to capitulate so that the other dimension may arise.

As for the radiance of the master, it is both beyond and at the heart of all his words and actions. It awakens in the disciple a force that annihilates all arrogance and also gives him the courage to look death in the face, the death of all that is not life, truth, and light within. This radiance is not sentimental but cutting, harsh and yet full of warmth; the master can be harsh in order to fill the other with beatitude and freedom.

The example of the master is never offered for imitation. His figure is original, unique and inimitable like the very life that he incorporates. That is what distinguishes him from false masters. Through what he says, his attitude and his way of being, he seeks only one thing: to provoke the disciple to his own reality, to reveal his originality, the inner master and Being which comes through him. He is not in any way the "good example" or the model, nor someone who knows more but, simply being himself, he witnesses to the transparence of the Transcendent.

Finally, shock is often one of the greatest means that the master utilizes: whether it be an absurd answer to a question, a sudden attack, a humiliation, a critique, a frightening yell or an ironic laugh. Everything is good for upsetting the established order, destroying the securities of the self, pulling the rug out from under its feet, and making it necessary to accept the unacceptable. "The way is narrow" which opens to the life. All that blocks and barricades it must be removed, all that holds us back must be abandoned, there is nothing which the master does not put into question. "Go, sell all you have. If someone wants to be my disciple, he must renounce himself and take up his cross and follow me."

AG : Life can only be transmitted through a living being, and he lights the fire in the heart of another only in the intensity of a personal relationship. It is a birth. The words of Christ which you cited show the requirements well and reveal, along with the entire

Gospel, that the tradition of the master is not only Eastern. It perpetuated itself during the first centuries at the heart of the teachings that were, after the "awakening," a time of "initiation" into the mysteries which culminated in baptismal "illumination"; the Churches constituted little communities developed and led by a "pastor," a spiritual master, whose unique goal was to "form the inner Christ," as Saint Paul said. And the same idea presided over primitive monasticism, which grouped a few monks around an ancient one or a "Father," someone who gave birth to life. Later, all this dried up as we wandered away from the source: baptism became a sociological rite, catechism teachers became professors of religion, the pastor became a notable administrator of a parish or lord of a diocese, the Father Abbot of a monastic order became a "Superior," and the Church became a "machine" according to the expression of the patriarch. Yet in Eastern Christianity, the tradition of the master remained uninterrupted; placing itself more in the line of Saint John the Mystic, it always had the "staretz," but they often had to be found in monasteries or some other secluded place. Nevertheless, in all the Churches we are now reacting against these historical crystallizations and the supremacy of the institution. A rebirth is taking place everywhere and there are many of us who wish to leap over fifteen centuries of history to finally recover the truth of our origins.

GD : Jesus Christ is the incarnation of the eternal master. He reunites in himself, in an absolutely unique way, all the traits that characterize the true master throughout all times and all countries. The moment has come to reunite with the great tradition of original Christianity, to rediscover its buried treasure of initiatiory knowledge and the experiential wisdom of the hermits and monks, along with all the mysticism that goes back to the Middle Ages.

In Jesus Christ, God seeks man; but man, unfortunately, has not always understood it that way.

AG : That is even how the Gospel begins: "He came among his own but his own did not receive him."

GD : Man puts God outside and erects himself as a god; through the autonomy of his own will and reason, he cuts himself off from his roots and loses his original ties with Being. That is the permanent destiny of man and he can be its victim even when he believes in God. Those people are rare who don't believe or accept anything that transcends their natural horizons. But who is this God they believe in? Very often, it is an almighty external power who is independent of man, but with whom he has alienating relations of submission and disobedience, to whom he runs when in despair, and who he invokes to obtain happiness and security. A useful god, but one whom we hold at a distance. Nevertheless, the divine Being continues to knock at our inner door, for transcendence is always immanent and desires to manifest itself in us and through us. Man does not enter into his true maturity and does not become true man except through this new consciousness. It explodes the image we have of ourselves, the one we created of God and of the relationship we have with Him.

It is always an overwhelming event in the life of man when he discovers that God is exterior because he put Him on the outside and holds the divine action at bay within him. The turning point occurs when he opens the door and ceases to resist that which is in his depths and that which he can become in his most secret core. He has then heard the voice of the inner Christ, but to follow Him on the way, he still needs a visible master, a guide.

AG : The Christian has no other master but Christ: "Call no one Master and Lord." The requirements of Jesus in relation to his disciples are unique. To follow him implies a total rupture with the past and an exclusive attachment to his person: sharing the same destiny as his; "carrying the cross," "drinking the cup" and receiving from him the Kingdom of Glory. To restrict this call of the master to a few privileged disciples is a profound error, which we have committed for centuries. The Fathers were categorical: "the Christ addresses himself to all men: the monk and the secular person must reach the same heights," says Saint John Chrysostom, among others. There is only one spirituality for all, without any distinction in its requirements.

The visible and external master remains necessary, and even indispensable in this context. Nevertheless, his only goal is to awaken the inner Christ in the other, not to imitate him, but to "put him on" and to "interiorize" him. This is a transmutation from which is born "the new man." "Awake you who sleep, awake from among the dead, and Christ will give you light." This theme, which runs throughout the primitive hymns, the Gospels and Saint Paul, was transmitted by the Fathers of the Church. It is a pleasure to find in Origen an emphasis on the *inbild* which you insist on so much in your works: to carry the "image" of Christ in oneself, to "image" his presence (*ein–bilden*) and in return the Christ transforms man into his own reality. "It is no longer I, but Christ who lives in me."

But something else seems essential to me: rare are those who have the opportunity to meet a real exterior master to show them the path. There the Christian tradition is firm: the master who guides us does not need to be a man. Most of the saints did not have one. For someone who is truly seeking, the masters are not lacking. Daily life, for example, is a place where the Word speaks constantly as the Fathers say. One needs the greatest intimacy with the "Bible which is the Christ in person," we must penetrate it and nourish ourselves from it, as with the eucharist, which is the summit of participation in Christ and union with him. That is why we consider the whole liturgy as the great master and the best teacher of the divine life. Nor should we forget personal prayer, of course, which structures and molds our being, carrying us to maturity and allowing "the Spirit itself to teach our hearts."

GD : It is certain that for the true disciple who has decided to advance on the way at all costs and to serve the life, life itself can become his master and each situation in daily life can be a test. His way of being in his body and his movements, his attitude in the present moment, all the highs and lows of his existence, the encounters, the unexpected events in life and the blows of destiny, the banalities and the great things. There is no moment or occasion through which we cannot hear the voice of the inner master or live before his gaze. As soon as we stagnate or deviate, he alerts us, he encourages and calls us when we hesitate to take the right road, or when we are afraid to take the leap. And when we are in the right attitude, an abyss of silence opens within us that has nothing to do with our usual psychological states: it is the beyond at the heart of life, and that master does not fail us, he is more available than any other and absolutely nothing escapes his vigilance.

The reading and reception of the Gospel offers man to the breath of God. The voice of the Holy Spirit that he perceives within makes him a disciple of the eternal master. Today we have entered an age witnessing a completely experiential discovery of the Spirit which inhabits us. Yet the person who continues to see the meaning of life in competition and comfort is still very far from it. There is an urgent need to penetrate the Bible other than through scientific and rational exegesis. If God is the beyond, an external comprehension of the texts will never allow us to discover the real content, and it is better to be silent. We must enter upon the way, unveil that which is hidden and become children of God, but nothing happens when we do it mentally or through some intellectual adherence. A living faith makes the believer listen to the mystery that speaks within and always opens him further to the truth of Christ. Then he must have antennas to hear the Word calling him in all places, and at every moment of the day. He experiences the presence of Christ as that of his eternal master; then the requirement to understand the world and love the other "in Christ" occurs by itself.

But to become transparent requires a ceaseless work on oneself, right into our least movements. The experience of the divine is, of course, a gift of grace and never the result of a man-made effort; but man must prepare himself actively, remain in the process of transformation and in state of continual watchfulness. We find here the third term of the inseparable triad: Master—Disciple—Way. The way begins only when the disciple has surrendered everything and has gone through two important stages of his evolution: where everything is centered on his ego; and where everything is centered on the other, a work or on the values of a community. Then he enters into a third stage where everything centers on the divine and on the transformation into a deified person. From that moment on the first two stages, the commitment toward oneself and the world, take on an entirely different meaning. The path signifies for the disciple an unconditional gift of self in following the master.

The path itself has two stages: first is the progressive letting go and the receiving of new life where the exercise of transformation for transparence is the way on the way; the second stage is when the man himself has become exercise and way, having attained the great Transparence that allows the divine to manifest itself without resistance. Then the way is the life in a human form and the truth of man is to go through it, in the image of Christ who said: "I am the Way, the Truth and the Life." There is never a point of arrival on this Way, it is itself its own goal.

AG : Becoming conscious that we are "illumined from the beginning," or that "the Kingdom of God is already within us" and that "we are resurrected as of now," according to the Christian tradition, can provoke an extraordinary relaxation, confidence and serenity in the person who seeks. In the end, we have neither to seek nor to wait for anything, but to let ourselves be seized. The Christ is "the beginning and the end, the Alpha and the Omega." In Him and with Him we are both on the way and already there, it is a life which never repeats itself twice and an always new truth which plunges us into the movement of ceaseless transformation.

GD : The way is not linear, but in the shape of a spiral, a leaning spiral where the circles fall into darkness and disappear in the heights of the light. At each revolution, it becomes more luminous. Its continual movement brings us to the periphery, from the external surface to the abysmal depths of the core and then back to the periphery. We are ceaselessly attracted toward the center, called by him, but at the same time sent outside. It is the very movement of the breath that inhabits us, and in its permanent coming and going we are completely penetrated from the most exterior layers to the deepest ones, and the deepest circles to the most exterior. We are deified.

But this incessant movement also opens the doors of humanity and of the cosmos. From our center, we rejoin all that surrounds us—people, objects, nature—from their periphery to their own center. In everything, Being that is within us recognizes Being that is in what is not us, and mysterious ties of profound relationship are woven beyond the seeming differences. Every external surface reflects in its depths the presence of our own Being that desires to manifest itself.

We can, unfortunately, let ourselves be caught up on the surface and remain stuck there, to our great loss. The movement does not tolerate any stagnation or fixation; it is a letting go, death and birth. We have only one thing to do: resist the temptation to direct the path ourselves. Any mixture of self is already a deviation which risks carrying us far from the center. Once we are on the way, we are seized and nothing else is asked of us but radical obedience.

The way is the eternal master as way. And when the disciple becomes the way, he himself becomes a master!

XI

"I will betroth you to myself for ever."
Hosea 2:19

.

GRAF DÜRCKHEIM: Among the great masters whom we can meet on the path of our existence, there is Love. It is the first enemy of our egotistical self, the movement par excellence of letting go and giving of self, the most fertile ground for the experience of Being. In love, the numinous is experienced to a degree that touches the whole of the person. To love is, above all, to feel unity.

Life is filled with passing moments in which we become "one" with an object, an animal, a person or God; occasions in which we can become conscious of a contact with Being. We can also experience Being in the absence and separation from something or someone who is dear to us; an unsatisfied desire to love or to be loved; or in solitude. Each time a profound yearning breaks over us and keeps our love from blossoming, we suffer from an ontological pain and can be seized by the divine. This does not happen only in exceptional situations, but in ordinary moments as well, such as a chance encounter with someone or something that goes beyond visible space and time. Love is in no way reduced to a feeling or a psychological process; this would be to remain on the surface. The person who has been drawn by a deeper consciousness and is attentive to its manifestation through the visible side of things sees his yearning for Being grow continuously, and discovers the possibility of uniting with it through everything. This is his great exercise on the path through daily life. But love can only take on its full dimension in the encounter with people. The true encounter between two people is very rare, but it occurs every time two beings meet each other in the presence of their essential Being. Then something specific happens in this union of the two on the level of their essence.

ALPHONSE GOETTMANN: Most of the time, the other appears under the painful weight of his existential self, with all the baggage of his history, the context of his relationships, his qualities and his weaknesses, and especially his social role, with which he easily risks being identified. To the extent that my own path is a journey, from my exterior toward my interior, I can join the other on the same path, and instead of judging him from the exterior, I call forth his own reality, sometimes even resurrect him. Our life is marked with such encounters; they are rare, but they are the ones that we owe everything to. It is not for nothing that Jesus was so severe toward those who judged others rather than opening them to their own transcendence. He taught us the gaze that plunges into the depths and overwhelms the heart.

GD : True love is realized when two persons, on the way toward the search for Being, find themselves and become companions on the road for each other. Their encounter becomes the path of their mutual fulfillment, if one hears the harmony of his own Being resonate in the other's heart. In no other place can we find such a thrill as in this communion from Being to Being. The sexual act between a man and woman is one of the summits of their union, that can take on an intensely mystical character and culminate in ecstasy. The couple can suddenly be carried toward another reality, absolutely beyond all dualism, and become liberated for a moment. If their attitude is right in the sexual exchange, each partner experiences a total letting go of self and, if they accept in surrender, the waters of life flood them completely and they are drowned, transcending their usual consciousness. It is the end of the egocentric self, and the union—the reciprocal "infusion" of the life of the two lovers, who experience a feeling of adoration for they are beyond space and time, seized by divine Being. They are reborn on an entirely new plane.

AG : It will take a long time to discover that vision, yet it is fundamentally biblical. Sexual love is not a conjunction of organs nor a copulation of two bodies: "Do you not know that your bodies are members of Christ?" Saint Paul cries out. When a man is united with a woman, "he is one body with her," and that is the Body of Christ.

The desecration of sexual love has always existed, but it was progressively introduced in the Church when it lost, particularly in the West, its interiority and its contemplative dimension. We then fell into the divisions of the mental—the categories of separation, the opposition between spiritual and physical—and we ended up making the sexual act a specific domain filled with ambiguity and suspicion. Only a person who lives from the contemplative experience can understand that sexual love calls for a contemplative approach that, far from being isolated, irradiates the whole field of human activity and offers a new attention to the world. Communion between two persons through the body is a communion with the whole of nature and the cosmos, which is the extension of our body. The exterior becomes interior.

GD : It is important to say that the depth of this openness depends entirely on the attitude of the one who lives the sexual act. We can let ourselves be caught up in erotic pleasure which is only a caricature of love—then we are lost. Man has a more difficult time than woman in this area, for he is often more objectifying, or keeps his distances instead of surrendering himself. But when the two consent to die in the other without resisting, a cosmic dizziness opens within them, the duality of their bodies are transcended through their union in an embrace where the love of God is manifested. We cannot be the same after such an experience. If love is truly the path for husband and wife, they are reborn each time on a new level of freedom. In marriage, it is not I, but the other who is the meaning of my life. The fruit of this total union is not the birth of a child, but the rebirth of the two partners in and through love. Love suffices to itself, there is no other goal. And its experience is once again a revelation of its triple aspect: fullness and power which emanate from all death of self; rebirth into another form and into an always new meaning; finally unity with the partner and harmony with the cosmic totality. The three are one in the eternal love which endlessly nourishes the movement of the lovers.

AG : At the risk of seeming foolish—although you took that risk with the Bible and the Fathers—we can say that a conjugal community can become a "theophany," the nuptial chamber of a covenant between God and humanity, a living icon of the Trinity. "Love is the fever of fire, the flame of the Lord," sings the Song of Songs. In each encounter with the beloved, it is the unique beloved which the lovers rediscover. According to Saint John Chrysostom, "Conjugal love is the most powerful love" because "it no longer seems like an earthly thing, but like the image of God himself." Humanity was created man and woman, their being is a "co-being," a single movement of one toward the other to become one, but without confusion or separation. They are two persons in a single being, continually engendered by a third: divine love, icon of the Trinity. But in recovering the paradisiacal state, the lovers are also a prophetic image of the Kingdom to come. They build the "House of God," as Clement of Alexandria says, and constitute the mystery of the Church, a "domestic Church," where the miracle of Cana is continued: water changed into wine, the world transmuted into its true reality, "all things become new," and the immense joy of the lovers hearing the voice of the Creator who presides over their wedding. Marriage is neither a biological fatality nor a remedy for concupiscence, but if it is going to be a spiritual path, it requires a harsh combat and an asceticism that is as intense as the efforts of the monks. In the Orthodox rite we crown the couple at the end of the celebration of the sacrament. They are "crowned with glory and honor," certainly, but also with the crown of thorns of their Lord and of the martyrs. There is no love without the cross.

GD : Many would like to stop time, to remain young forever. Yet, "the Being of God is our becoming," said Meister Eckhart; it is therefore in remaining in becoming that the divine Being manifests itself to us and that we realize our vocation as human beings! The one who is not afraid of aging is also crowned by life, for age does not so much signify a catastrophic end, but the true wedding of man with his eternal nature. To say "yes" to old age is to enter into the fullness of maturity, the opposite of a sad and painful regression, or of a grim waiting for death. But this obviously assumes that we sink our roots into a reality that is beyond the opposites "young and old," and that we experience its presence precisely through becoming and the transitional.

The old person is affected in the highest degree by the triple distress of which we have spoken: his vital force is abandoning him physically and spiritually; his life seems to have no more meaning because it is useless and of little productive value; and finally, he feels himself invaded by inevitable solitude. But if he is truly wedded to the path, he knows that he is affected only on the surface of his most exterior self, and that a reduction of his natural forces

Dürckheim with students at Béthanie

actually favors the arising of his supernatural powers, whose blossoming is the ultimate achievement of his existence. If he refuses to age and hides from himself and others the signs of his age by fighting with all sorts of security methods, he misses the last and most beautiful gift that life can give him. This man only sees the oppressive shadow of his aging swallowing up the remainder of his days. But the one who has awakened to the other way of seeing contemplates, on the horizon of his life, the rising sun that announces for him a new age. Far from stagnating in death's waiting room, letting go more than ever of all the worldly ties that pulled him toward the exterior, he now makes great strides on the path of incessant transformation. Something absolutely new can visit him, and the veil that separates him from the invisible becomes transparent in the extreme. Perhaps his backbone is curved by the weight of years, but nothing can take his joy away, not even death, which is at his side like an old companion in whom he confides.

Instead of being a poison for the whole family, a tyrant in the house and a burden to everyone—as is the case most of the time—this old man is a light to his entourage, secretly attracting others by his radiance. He is admired and loved for the ineffable emanation coming from him. He has found genuine youth.

AG : That youth is always before us. It is that within us which has no age at all. Perhaps is it God Himself, eternal youth.

GD : That is why this old man is a sage. He no longer looks behind him with bitterness toward the fleeting youth of another time. He is breaking through time and crossing over it. His wisdom has nothing to do with power, knowledge or possession. Whatever knowledge he may have accumulated over his long life, it is no longer his support; what he contemplates from now on cannot be conceived of and escapes all reasoning. He has only a silent smile to express himself. This man does not age, he matures; his triple distress is the place of a triple manifestation: he is wise; he radiates; he is good. This is Being under its three aspects.

AG : Western civilization is not sensitive to all this, and sees no interest in it. Man is an animal of production and when he ceases to be useful, he is rejected. To the eternal question of Tolstoy: "What makes men live?" the system answers: "Work, mechanization, ideology." And if they have any pleasures left where the thirst for eternity comes to the surface, the society of consumption buys it through its "little eternities of delights" as Kierkegaard ironically said.

GD : In the East it is said: "An old man who is bitter is a ridiculous person," and when people are asked about the treasure of their civilization, they answer: "It is first of all our elderly." Old people should normally have gone through the stages of the path, their whole being should be grounded in the only reality that really interests man—they should hold the secret of life. In this case, radiance is the real fruit of the maturity of the elderly and replaces activity. Who to turn to but them, if we do not wish to bypass the real?

AG : Hopefully, the day will come when we will no longer push our elderly into institutions. For the moment, they are still our "Achilles' heel," the weak side of our humanity where death never ceases to gnaw at us and spread terror in our hearts. The specter of death has become the new taboo in modern societies. As soon as it arises, we quickly get rid of it, after having painted it up and covered it with flowers to forget its livid face. We believe with the Epicurians that death does not concern us: "As long as we are alive, it is not there; and when we die, it is we who are no longer there."

GD : Initiated man—that is to say, the one who has opened the door to mystery—knows that death is always there and that we are born with it. To die and to be born go together for an individual on the path. Death will not eliminate him, but makes him grow beyond himself into eternal birth. In this encounter he hears the definite call of the master who invites us one last time to remove the clothing of the multiple and enter into the fullness of unity. Yet, instead of veiling death and turning our back on it, we must learn to look at it at length and in silence. If the sight of a corpse does not always cause panic and horror, it nevertheless makes everyone silent, for it goes beyond our understanding: there is nothing more to say or to think. Alone in this silence of death we can hear the voice of the master who seeks to speak to us.

In the end, are we afraid of death, or of the power of life that surges up at the moment of death? The meaning that we give to death depends on the meaning that we give to life, and both depend on the stage of our inner evolution. For someone who has built his life on prestige and possessions, death is a constant menace and a tragic failure; for the one whose life is Being, death is its ultimate unveiling. He also passes through the pangs and

Dürckheim with students

anguish, but he holds on for he senses the glow of the infinite which soon comes to remove all limits and to project him into the light without end. For him, the meaning of death is life, and he alone truly lives who knows how to die. Only if we feel death within us can we also feel the life to which it opens us. Instead of being a horror, death can become the mysterious friend of our steps along the way, where there is finally no joy without it.

Seen from the exterior death is an end, but seen from within it is a beginning. Whether we wish it or not, it is the inevitable letting go of everything, the surrender to and union with the fullness of the original depths. From this union is born true individuality. This movement of transformation is also the only true meditation that introduces the seriousness of final death into the context of the partial deaths of daily life. Every time the natural self dies a little and gives way, man enters more deeply into contact with his essence and the life from which can be born a self that is not of this world. There is no transformation without "un-becoming." Humanity's eternal question is this: how to live fully, how to let rise within oneself the living push of Being; how to arrive at the true Life that resonates in our depths? The eternal answer is: only through death. To die is a grim prospect only for he who is a prisoner of his mundane self. For the awakened, the disciple on the path of initiation, it is the natural condition of an attitude which allows the advent of the unconditioned. Among certain people, dying is so natural that they do not even speak of "living and dying," but of "living and being born again."

AG : On this subject, Christians from the West are rather paganized. Yet after the overwhelming news of Christ resurrected, the tragedy of death disappeared. We no longer spoke of "the day of death," but of the "day of birth"—*dies natalis*—and the martyrs went singing into the arena. From then on the whole Church was founded on the Easter event. The resurrection was introduced not only into human hearts, but into all of human and cosmic history in order to communicate to all and everything the divine life of the Trinity. Baptism had already begun this supreme trans-figuration, and death achieved it as the great passage toward ultimate metamorphosis.

We seek today to renew this ancient tradition. The concrete experience of Christ dead and resurrected is lived through the way of the liturgical seasons and the ecclesiastical community. Through victory over death and this wondrous eruption of life, Easter has again become for us the feast of feasts, an overflowing joy that is indescribable to the person who has not lived it. The Christ our life is here, palpable and real, bearing witness to the fact that we will not die. But this feast and this joy is reiterated at each eucharist and finally it becomes intimate to us in every meditation. "O death, where is thy sting?"

GD : Death is the great life always at work. It is not the enemy, but the friend who gives us a hand to pass over the threshold toward our wedding with Being, and enter into a country which we have never left.

Chronology

1896   Birth of Karlfried Graf Dürckheim in Munich.

1914 - 1918   On the front during the First World War.

1918 - 1923   Studies in philosophy and psychology at Munich and Kiel. Doctorate in Philosophy.

1925 - 1932   Assistant in the Institute of Psychology at the University of Leipzig.

1930   Doctorate in Psychology.

1932   Professor of Psychology at the Academy of Pedagogy and Philosophy at the University of Kiel.

1937 - 1947   Mission and research in Japan.

1948 - 1988   Psychotherapist with colleagues in Todtmoos-Rütte (Black Forest) where he founded a "Center of Existential and Psychological Formation and Encounter."

December 1988   Death at the age of ninety-two at Todtmoos.

A Dürckheim Bibliography

English Translations:

1. *Zen and Us,* E.P. Dutton, New York, 1987.

2. *The Way of Transformation: Daily Life as Spiritual Exercise,* Allen & Unwin, London, 1988.

3. *Hara: The Vital Center of Man,* Allen & Unwin, London, 1984.

4. *The Call For the Master: The Meaning of Spiritual Guidance on the Way to the Self,* E.P. Dutton, New York, 1989.

French Translations:

5. *La Percée de L'être,* Ed. Le Courier du Livre, Paris, 1971.

6. *L'homme et sa Double Origine,* Ed. du Cerf, Paris, 1976.

7. *Exercises Initiatique dans la Psychothérapie,* Ed. Le Courrier du Livre, Paris, 1977.

8. *Méditer—Pourquoi et Comment?* Ed. Le Courrier du Livre, Paris, 1978.

9. *L'expérience de la Transcendance,* Ed. Le Courrier du Livre, Paris, 1987.

10. *L'esprit Guide,* Albin Michel, Paris, 1975.

In German:

11. *Erlebnis und Wandlung.* Ed. Otto-Wilhelm Barth, 2nd edition, Munich, 1978.

12. *Wunderbare Katze,* Ed. Otto-Wilhem Barth, 3rd edition, Munich 1975.

13. *Uberweltliches Leben in der Welt,* Ed.Otto-Wilhelm Barth, 2nd edition, Munich 1972.

14. *Der Rul Nach Dem Meister*, Ed. Otto-Wihelm Barth, 2nd edition, Munich 1975.

15. *Im Zeichen der Grossen Erfahrung*, Ed. Otto-Wilhelm Barth, 3rd edition, Munich 1974.

16. *Japan und die Kultur der Stille*, Ed. Otto-Wilhelm Barth, 6th edition, Munich 1975.

17. *Mächtigkeit, Rang und Stufe*, Ed. Aurum, Fribourg 1978.

18. *Sportliche Leistung - Menschliche Reife*, Ed. Wilhelm Limpert, 3rd edition, Frankfort, 1969.

In French:

19. *Graf Dürckheim - Dialogue sur le Chemin Initiatique*, Dervy Livres, Paris, 1984.

20. *Regards Inédits sur Graf Dürckheim*, Editions Béthanie, Gorze, 1990.

21. *Mémoire éternelle pour Graf Dürckheim*, Dervy Livres, Paris, 1990.

To be published:

The Beyond Within: Initiation into Meditation, Abbey Press, Saint Meinrad, 1992.

More spiritual classics
from Globe Press Books

The Body of Light
History and Practical Techniques for Awakening Your Subtle Body
by John Mann and Lar Short.
A concise guide to the use of chakras for self-development. Reviews Hindu, Buddhist, Taoist and other traditions, and includes beginning, intermediate and advanced exercises, with over 60 illustrations. 1990. 192 pages, softcover, $12.95.

The Training of the Zen Buddhist Monk
by D.T. Suzuki.
This is perhaps the best introduction to Zen and the life of the Zen monk. Forty-three illustrations by the monk Zenchu Sato depict many common practices in the life of the monks. 1991. 176 pages, 43 illustrations. Softcover, $9.95.

On A Spaceship With Beelzebub
By A Grandson of Gurdjieff
by David Kherdian.
A noted author tells the story of his own journey into and through the powerful Gurdjieff work of inner transformation. 1991. 288 pages. Hardcover, $24.95. Softcover, $12.95.

Self-Remembering
by Robert Earl Burton.
A contemporary teacher of the Fourth Way shows the relation of self-remembering to every phase of the student's life and work. 1991. 232 pages. Hardcover, $40.00.

New Horizons
Explorations in Science
by P.D. Ouspensky.

Explore the outer reaches of science with one of this century's greatest thinkers. Reprinted from *A New Model of the Universe*, these essays explain new outlooks on physics, the fourth dimension, mystical states of consciousness, and the study of dreams and hypnotism. With a new Introduction by Colin Wilson. 1990. 222 pages, softcover, $14.95.

The Wisdom of Sri Nisargadatta Maharaj
by Robert Powell.

The best introduction to the life and profound teachings of Nisargadatta. Includes many penetrating aphorisms, a biographical sketch, details of Nisargadatta's life, and commentary by Powell, author of *Zen and Reality*. 1992. 128 pages, softcover, $10.95.

Look Inside
by Cathy London.

A woman's personal thoughts on discovering herself and learning to successfully cope with the conflicts of a relationship. A beautiful gift book, 1991. 96 pages, softcover, $8.95.

Body Types
The Enneagram of Essence Types
by Joel Friedlander.

Learn how to recognize the physical and psychological tendencies of each type. Explore the automatic thoughts, attitudes and motives of your type, and discover the dynamics behind your relationships. 1986. 192 pages, Softcover, $10.95.

Available at fine bookstores, or order direct from the publisher.
To order or request a free catalog, send check, money order or
complete Visa/MasterCard information and signature, along
with $1.50 per item for shipping to:
Globe Press Books
P.O. Box 2045, Madison Station
New York, NY 10159.